MADRID

TOP SIGHTS · LOCAL EXPERIENCES

ANTHONY HAM

Contents

Plan Your Trip

Statue of Felipe III, Plaza Mayor (p36)
MATTEO COLOMBO / GETTY IMAGES ©

Explore Madrid · 33

Worth a Trip

Survival Guide · 145

Special Features

Welcome to Madrid

No city on earth is more alive than Madrid, a beguiling place whose sheer energy carries a simple message: this is one city that knows how to live. Madrid's calling cards are many: astonishing art galleries, stunning architecture, relentless nightlife, fine restaurants and tapas bars. Other cities have some of these things. Madrid has them all in bucketloads.

The Edificio Metrópolis (p72) marks the southern end of Gran Vía.

Top Sights

Museo del Prado

Among the world's finest galleries. **p86**

SEAN PAVONE/SHUTTERSTOCK ©

JOAQUÍN CORTÉS/ROMAN LORES. IMAGE COURTESY OF CATARINA BELOVA/SHUTTERSTOCK ©

Centro de Arte Reina Sofía

Picasso, Dalí and Miró. **p96**

Parque del Buen Retiro

Magnificent monumental parklands. **p100**

DAM EASTLAND / ALAMY STOCK PHOTO ©

Museo Thyssen-Bornemisza

Fabulous collection of European art. **p92**

Palacio Real
Palatial royal architectural showpiece. **p38**

Ermita de San Antonio de la Florida
The splendour of Goya's frescoes. **p138**

Museo Lázaro Galdiano
Salamanca's noblest art-filled mansion. **p108**

Plaza Mayor
Madrid's grandest public square. **p36**

Plaza de Toros
An architecturally splendid bullring. **p120**

San Lorenzo de El Escorial
Unesco-listed royal extravagance. **p140**

Restaurants

It's not that the Madrid's culinary traditions are anything special. Rather, everything that is exciting about Spanish cooking finds expression in the capital, from Basque tapas bars to avant garde Catalan chefs, from the best in Galician seafood to Andalucía's Mediterranean catch. Travel from one Spanish village to the next and you'll learn that each has its own speciality. Travel to Madrid and you'll find them all.

Madrid Specialties

The city's traditional local cuisine is dominated by hearty stews, particularly in winter, and there are none more hearty than *cocido a la madrileña*, a hotpot or stew that starts with a noodle broth and is followed by, or combined with, carrots, chickpeas, chicken, *morcilla* (blood sausage), beef, lard and possibly other sausage meats, too. Other popular staples include *cordero asado* (roast lamb), *croquetas* (croquettes), *patatas con huevos fritos* (baked potatoes with eggs, also known as *huevos rotos*), *tortilla dc patatas* (a thick potato omelette) and endless variations on *bacalao* (cod).

Regional Specialties

Madrid's local cuisine is only half the story. The city has also wholeheartedly embraced dishes – and the innovations that accompany them – from across the country. Most notably, every day tonnes of fish and seafood are trucked in from Mediterranean and Atlantic ports to satisfy the *madrileño* (a resident of Madrid) taste for the sea to the extent that, remarkably for a city so far inland, Madrid is home to the world's second-largest fish market (after Tokyo).

Best for Local Cooking

Taberna La Bola One of the best places in town to try *cocido a la madrileña* and other local favourites such as *callos* (tripe). (p45)

Malacatín A tiled bar where the *cocido* can be tried as a tapas or the more authentic all-you-can-eat version. (p58)

CASSANDRA GAMBILL/LONELY PLANET ©

Restaurante Sobrino de Botín The world's oldest restaurant and a hugely atmospheric place to sample roasted meats. (p83)

Lhardy The great and the good of Madrid, from royalty to A-list celebrities, have all eaten in this bastion of traditional cooking. (Pictured above; p76)

Posada de la Villa Another historical converted inn where the roasted meats have acquired legendary status across the city. (p60)

Casa Lucio One of Madrid's most celebrated restaurants, where royalty and ordinary *madrileños* order *cocido* and the city's best *huevos rotos*. (p58)

Best for Regional Spanish

Maceiras Earthy decor and good down-home cooking from the coasts of Galicia – *pulpo* (octopus) is the prize dish. (p74)

La Cocina de María Luisa The inland cuisine of Castilla y León takes centre stage at this well-regarded Salamanca eatery. (p116)

Biotza The best in Basque cooking from bite-sized *pintxos* (Basque tapas) to sit-down meals out back. (p116)

A Culinary Experience 🍽

DiverXo (☏91 570 07 66; www.diverxo.com; Calle de Padre Damián 23; set menus €195-250; ⏱2-3.30pm & 9-10.30pm Tue-Sat, closed three weeks in Aug; Ⓜ Cuzco) in northern Madrid is the city's only three-Michelin-starred restaurant. Chef David Muñoz favours what he calls a 'brutal' approach to cooking – his team of chefs appear mid-bite to add surprising new ingredients.

Tapas

The art of ir de tapear (going out for tapas) is one of Madrid's most enduring and best-loved gastronomic and social traditions rolled into one. Many of the city's best tapas bars clamour for space in La Latina, but such is the local love of tapas that every Madrid barrio (district) has some fabulous options.

MATT MUNRO/LONELY PLANET ©

Best for Tapas

Estado Puro Madrid's most innovative tapas from the kitchen lab of masterchef Paco Roncero. (p104)

Taberna Matritum Slightly removed from the main La Latina tapas zone, but worth the slight detour. (p58)

Juana La Loca Wins our vote for Madrid's best *tortilla de patatas* (Spanish omelette). (p58)

Txirimiri Fantastic *tortilla de patatas* and so much more, with a Basque theme for much of what's on offer. (p57)

Casa Alberto Tapas like *jamón* and *croquetas* as they used to be in a traditional setting. (p74)

Pez Tortilla *Tortilla de patatas*, *croquetas* and craft beer. (p128)

Casa Revuelta A Madrid institution for the city's best cod bites, as well as tripe and bacon bits. (p44)

Bocaito Classic Andalucian tapas, and bar staff who keep things loud and ticking over. (p130)

Mercado de San Miguel Fresh produce market meets delicatessen with some of Madrid's most desirable tapas. (Pictured above; p44)

Cafes

Madrid's thriving cafe culture dates back to the early to mid-20th century, when old-style coffeehouses formed the centrepiece of the country's intellectual life. Many have been lost to time, but some outstanding examples remain and their clientele long ago broadened to encompass an entire cross-section of modern Madrid society. Most of the cafes covered here are primarily places to take a coffee at any hour of the day and we recommend them as such.

VICTOR TORRES/SHUTTERSTOCK ©

Best Old Literary Cafes

Café-Restaurante El Espejo Another of the grand old dames of Madrid high society, this storied cafe retains its original decor. (p131)

Café Comercial One of the city's oldest cafes located on Glorieta de Bilbao. (p131)

Gran Café de Gijón The third in a triumvirate of cafes that rank among Europe's best. (p131)

Cafe de Oriente Fabulous palace views and a stately Central European feel. (p47)

Best Meeting Places

Café Manuela Old-world decoration and the lively hum of modern Madrid – a perfect mix. (p132)

Café del Real Cool and intimate urban space in the heart of the city. (p47)

Lolina Vintage Café One of Malasaña's coolest retro cafes, with coffee, cocktails and a mixed crowd. (p125)

Shopping

Madrid is a great place to shop, and shopping in the Spanish capital often involves debunking a few stereotypes. Fashionistas will discover a whole new world of designers. The buzz surrounding Spanish food and drink is not restricted to the city's restaurants and tapas bars, as there are some fine purveyors of gourmet foods where you can shop for goodies to carry back home. And then there are the antiques and quality souvenirs.

Spanish Fashions

Just as Spanish celebrity chefs have taken the world by storm, the world's most prestigious catwalks are clamouring for Spanish designers. The bold colours and eye-catching designs may be relative newcomers on the international stage, but they've been around in Madrid for far longer, with most designers making their names during the creative outpouring of *la movida madrileña* (the Madrid scene) in the 1980s.

Gourmet Foods

Madrid's markets have undergone something of a revolution in recent years, transforming themselves into vibrant spaces where you can eat as well as shop. Added to these are the small specialist stores where the packaging is often as exquisite as the tastes on offer.

Antiques & Souvenirs

You could buy your friends back home a bullfighting poster with their names on it. Or you could go for a touch more class and take home a lovely papier mâché figurine, a carefully crafted ceramic bowl or a hand-painted Spanish fan.

Best for Spanish Fashions

Agatha Ruiz de la Prada The icon of a generation, Agatha's outrageous colours make her the Pedro Almodóvar of Spanish fashion. (Pictured above; p111)

Camper Only Spanish designers could make a world fashion superstar out of bowling-shoe chic. (p111)

Manolo Blahnik The world-famous maker of designer shoes for celebrities from all corners of the globe. (p111)

INGOLF POMPE 85 / ALAMY STOCK PHOTO ©

Best for Gourmet Foods

Mercado de San Miguel Cured meats all vacuum-sealed and ready to take home is just one of the things this remodelled market does so well. (p44)

Bombonerías Santa Old-style and near-perfect chocolates gift-wrapped like works of art. (p119)

Oriol Balaguer One of Spain's most celebrated pastry chefs is also a chocolatier par excellence. (p119)

Mantequería Bravo The best old-style Spanish deli in Madrid. (p118)

Best for Antiques & Souvenirs

El Arco Artesanía Designer souvenirs from papier mâché to ceramics and scarves right on Plaza Mayor. (p48)

Antigua Casa Talavera Ceramics and tileworks with an individual touch from family potters across the Spanish interior. (p48)

Casa Hernanz Rope-soled *alpargatas* (espadrilles) footwear is the perfect souvenir of the Spanish summer. (p48)

Maty Flamenco dresses and shoes that have the stamp of authenticity. (p49)

Botería Julio Rodríguez Old Spanish wineskins as they used to be. (p62)

Art

Madrid is one of the great art capitals of the world. The city's astonishing collection of art museums is the legacy of self-aggrandising Spanish royals of centuries past who courted the great painters of the day and built up peerless collections of masterpieces from all across Europe.

The Golden Mile

Few streets on the planet have the artistic pedigree of the Paseo del Prado. Arrayed along (or just set back from) its shores are three of the world's best art galleries, known locally as the Prado, Thyssen and Reina Sofía. Together their collections form a catalogue of breathtaking breadth and richness, spanning the generations of Spanish masters from Goya to Picasso, with all the major European masters thrown in for good measure.

Beyond the Paseo del Prado

In the rush to Madrid's big three art museums, visitors too often neglect (or fail to realise that they're alongside) other galleries that would be major attractions in any other city. These include one of the few places where Goya's paintings remain in their original setting; an art college where all the Spanish greats studied; and a gallery devoted entirely to Joaquín Sorolla, one of Spain's most admired painters but little known beyond Spanish shores. And from the Prado and Reina Sofía to the Caixa Forum and Museo Sorolla, the buildings in which these collections hang rank among Madrid's most artistic architectural forms.

Best for Spanish Masters

Museo del Prado Come for Goya and Velázquez, but stay all day for a journey through the richest centuries of European art. A worthy rival to the Louvre – it's that good. (p86)

Real Academia de Bellas Artes de San Fernando Picasso and Dalí studied here, and there are works

by Goya, Picasso, Velázquez and Zurbarán to name just some of the household names you'll find here. (p71)

Ermita de San Antonio de la Florida Extraordinary frescoes painted by Goya in 1798 remain *in situ* in this unassuming little hermitage – one of Madrid's most underrated attractions. (p138)

Best for Contemporary Art

Centro de Arte Reina Sofía Picasso's *Guernica* and the artist's preparatory sketches steal the show, but there's also Salvador Dalí, Joan Miró and the leading artists of 20th-century Spain. (p96)

Caixa Forum Avant-garde architecture provides the stage for a rich and revolving round of temporary exhibitions across a range of genres that include photography, painting and installation art. (p103)

Best of the Rest

Museo Thyssen-Bornemisza Private collection that encompasses the great names of European art, beginning in medieval times and reaching a crescendo with Jackson Pollock and Mark Rothko. (Pictured above; p92)

Museo Sorolla Valencian artist whose paintings (and former home that houses them) capture the essence of the Mediterranean. (p137)

Museo Lázaro Galdiano Another stellar private collection with Goya, El Greco and Constable in a fine old Salamanca mansion. (p108)

Real Monasterio de San Lorenzo El Greco and so many other minor masters add art gallery to this palace-monastery complex's myriad charms. (p140)

Green Spaces

The most obvious choice for an escape into Madrid's greenery is the Parque del Buen Retiro, one of Europe's loveliest parks and monumental gardens, but there are plenty of other options. The footpaths running down the middle of the Paseo del Prado are gloriously shady, presided over by trees planted in the 18th century, and lined on one side by the Real Jardín Botánico, Madrid's botanical gardens.

ITZAVU/SHUTTERSTOCK ©

Best Parks

Parque del Buen Retiro
Madrid's loveliest and largest stand of green, dotted with monuments and filled with empty lawns. (p100)

Jardines de Sabatini
Manicured gardens in the shadow of the Palacio Real, with fountains and maze-like hedges. (p39)

Plaza de Olavide One of Madrid's greenest squares, with shaded bars around the perimeter. (p137)

Real Jardín Botánico
Pathways wind between vast stands of plants, exotic and otherwise, a few steps from the Museo del Prado in the heart of town. (Pictured above; p103)

Best Beyond the Centre

Casa de Campo A vast parkland west of downtown Madrid, with restaurants, a cable car, lake, zoo and fun park.

Campo del Moro The Retiro's rival for the title of Madrid's loveliest park – it's hidden down the hill behind the royal palace.

For Kids

Like all major cities, Madrid requires you to plan carefully to make sure that your children enjoy their visit to the city as much as you do. The major art galleries sometimes have activities for children, while most also have printed guides to their collections designed for them. Public playgrounds also inhabit many city squares – ask the tourist office if they know the nearest one, and the Parque del Buen Retiro has a host of child-centric activities on offer.

EDACCORA/SHUTTERSTOCK ©

Best for Kids

Parque del Buen Retiro
Playgrounds, vast open spaces, boat rides, bike hire and occasional puppet shows. (Pictured above; p100)

Zoo Aquarium de Madrid
An attractive zoo with a full range of species in Casa de Campo. (☎902 345014; www.zoomadrid.com; adult/child €23/19; ☺10.30am-10pm Sun-Thu, to midnight Fri & Sat Jul & Aug, shorter hours Sep-Jun; ☒37 from Intercambiador de Príncipe Pío, Ⓜ Casa de Campo)

Parque de Atracciones
A good amusement park with plenty of rides for all ages. (☎91 463 29 00; www.parquedeatracciones. es; adult/child €32/25; ☺noon-midnight Jul & Aug, hours vary Sep-Jun).

Teleférico A trundling cable car that connects the Paseo de Pinto Rosales to Casa de Campo. (☎91 541 11 18; www.teleferico.com; cnr Paseo del Pintor Rosales & Calle de Marqués de Urquijo; one-way/return €4.20/5.90; ☺noon-9pm May-Aug, reduced hours Sep-Apr; Ⓜ Argüelles)

Estadio Santiago Bernabéu Home of Real Madrid and one of the most impressive football stadiums on earth, with tours, a museum, and matches from August to May. (☎902 324324; www.realmadrid. com; Avenida de Concha Espina 1; tickets from €40; Ⓜ Santiago Bernabéu)

Casa Museo de Ratón Perez Guided visits for kids through the home of Spain's version of the tooth fairy. (☎91 522 69 68; www. casamuseoratonperez.com; 1st fl, Calle de Arenal 8; €3; ☺5-8pm Mon, 11am-2pm)

Bars

Nights in the Spanish capital are the stuff of legend and what Ernest Hemingway wrote of the city in the 1930s remains true to this day: 'Nobody goes to bed in Madrid until they have killed the night.' Madrid has more bars than any city in the world, six, in fact, for every 100 inhabitants, and wherever you are in town, there'll be a bar close by.

Pre-Dinner Drinks

If you're unaccustomed to Madrid's late eating hours, the upside is that it allows plenty of time for a pre-dinner drink, an activity that locals have turned into an institution. Of course, they often combine the two – eating and drinking – by starting early with a drink and some tapas. So in addition to the bars we cover in these lists, it's always worth considering those places better known for their food when planning your first step into the night because they're often terrific places to drink as well.

Opening Hours

Madrid's bars range from simple, local watering holes that serve as centres of community life to sophisticated temples to good taste. The former are usually open throughout the day, while the latter rarely open before 8pm. Otherwise, some places may close half an hour earlier or later (especially on Friday and Saturday nights), but 3am operates as a threshold. The hours between midnight and 3am are filled with choices, although we recommend that you take up residence in one of the oh-so-cool cocktail bars.

Best Cocktail Bars

Museo Chicote Madrid's most famous cocktail bar, beloved by celebrities from Hemingway to Sophia Loren. (p131)

Del Diego A quieter venue for A-list *famosos* (celebrities), with near-perfect (and always creative) cocktails. (p132)

1862 Dry Bar Inventive cocktails in sophisticated surrounds down on happening Calle del Pez. (p132)

CASSANDRA GAMBILL/LONELY PLANET ©

Rooftop Bars

La Terraza del Urban The height of class on a warm summer's evening. (p77)

Tartân Roof Slick venue high above one of Madrid's prettiest corners. (p76)

Old Barrio Bars

La Venencia A timeless sherry bar where old barrels abound, close to Plaza de Santa Ana. (p76)

Bodega de la Ardosa Another neighbourhood classic, in Malasaña. (Pictured above; p129)

Best of the Rest

Café Belén Chilled bar staff, chilled punters and fabulous mojitos. (p131)

Delic Wonderful setting on a medieval square and mojitos of the highest order. (p60)

El Imperfecto Great cocktails and a real Huertas buzz make this one of Madrid's best bars. (p76)

Taberna El Tempranillo A great La Latina wine bar along Calle de la Cava Baja, with an entire wall of wine bottles. (p60)

Anticafé Bohemian decor and an alternative slant on life. (p47)

Taberna La Dolores Classy and historic bar in the Paseo del Prado hinterland. (p69)

For the Love of the Game

Overlooking one of the most famous football fields on earth, the **Real Café Bernabéu** (☏91 458 36 67; www.realcafe bernabeu.es; Gate 30, Estadio Santiago Bernabéu, Avenida de Concha Espina; ⏰10am-2am; Ⓜ Santiago Bernabéu) is a trendy cocktail bar with exceptional views and a steady stream of beautiful people among the clientele. It closes two hours before a game and doesn't open until an hour after.

Live Music & Flamenco

Madrid has a happening live-music scene, which owes a lot to the city's role as the cultural capital of the Spanish-speaking world. There's flamenco, world-class jazz and a host of performers you may never have heard of – one of whom may just be Spain's next big thing. For something more edifying, there's opera and zarzuela (Spanish mix of theatre, music and dance).

Flamenco

Flamenco's roots lie in Andalucía, but the top performers gravitate towards Madrid for live performances; in June, Madrid hosts the prestigious **Suma Flamenca festival** (www.madrid.org/sumaflamenca). Remember also that most *tablaos* (flamenco venues) offer meals to go with the floorshow. In our experience, the meals are often overpriced, but if you just pay for the show (the admission usually includes a drink), you may not have the best seat in the house. If possible, buy your ticket in person at the venue to get a sense of where you'll be seated.

Jazz

Madrid has some of Europe's best jazz, with at least three fine venues. Groups often play for a whole week, making it easier to get tickets.

Rock Madrid

At the height of *la movida madrileña*, the crazy outpouring of creativity and hedonism in Madrid in the 1980s, an estimated 300 rock bands were performing in the bars of Malasaña alone. There aren't quite so many these days, but there are still plenty that capture that spirit.

Best Flamenco

Teatro Flamenco Madrid Fantastic new theatre stage with reasonable prices and high-quality flamenco. (p133)

Las Tablas A smaller, more intimate venue with consistently excellent performances. (p47)

Casa Patas One of Madrid's most celebrated flamenco stages, with a respected flamenco school attached. (p61)

EFIRED/SHUTTERSTOCK ©

Villa Rosa Once appeared in an Almodóvar movie and has recently returned to its flamenco roots. (p80)

Café de Chinitas A fine stage with an elegant setting. (p47)

Café Ziryab One of the best places in Madrid for improvised flamenco. (p62)

Best Jazz

Café Central Regularly ranked among the elite of world jazz clubs; all the big names have played beneath the fabulous art deco decor. (p78)

El Junco Jazz Club Live jazz then dancing all night: it's a fine combination. (p135)

Best Rock & the Rest

Sala El Sol One of the legends of 1980s Madrid and still going strong. (p78)

Costello Café & Niteclub A sophisticated venue that feels like a SoHo cocktail bar. (p80)

ContraClub Rock is often part of a diverse mix at this live-music-venue-slash-club. (p62)

Best High Culture

Teatro Real Spain's finest opera performers take to the stage at this acoustically perfect venue. (Pictured above; p43)

Teatro de la Zarzuela Madrid's very own cross between theatre and opera; the theatre also hosts the finest in contemporary dance. (p78)

Clubs

Madrid nights are long and loud and people here live fully for the moment. Today's encounter can be tomorrow's distant memory, perhaps in part because Madrid's nightclubs (also known as discotecas) rival any in the world. The best places are usually the mega-clubs with designer decor, designer people and, sometimes, with enough space for numerous dance floors each with their own musical style to suit your mood.

MARK READ/LONELY PLANET ©

Opening Hours & Admission

Most nightclubs don't open their doors until around midnight, don't really get going until after 1am, and some won't even bat an eyelid until 3am, when the bars elsewhere have closed. Admission prices vary widely, but the standard admission costs around €15. Even those that let you in for free will play catch-up with hefty drinks prices, so don't plan your night around looking for the cheapest ticket.

Best Clubs

Teatro Joy Eslava Enduringly popular converted theatre with great music, live acts and a fun crowd. (p45)

Teatro Kapital Madrid's megaclub of longest standing with seven floors and something for everyone. (p105)

Ya'sta Thirty years on, this Malasaña epic just keeps rolling on into the night. (p133)

Almonte Flamenco tunes and a formidable cast of amateur flamenco wannabes make for an alternative slant to the night. (p118)

Gabana 1800 Keep your eyes peeled for the Real Madrid set; it has a tough door policy, as you'd expect. (p117)

For Free

BILL PERRY/SHUTTERSTOCK ©

Madrid can be expensive, but with careful planning, the combination of free attractions and specific times when major sights offer free entry enables you to see the best the city has to offer without burning a large hole in your pocket.

Best Always-Free Places

Ermita de San Antonio de la Florida Goya's frescoes are free, just where he painted them. (p138)

El Rastro The Sunday-morning flea market is one of Madrid's premier attractions. (p53)

Parque del Buen Retiro One of Europe's grandest, most beautiful city parks. (p100)

Estación de Chamberí Take a journey underground to Madrid's ghost metro station. (p137)

Templo de Debod Madrid's very own Egyptian temple doesn't cost a cent, nor does the lovely parkland that surrounds it. (p139)

Museo al Aire Libre Outdoor sculptures by some of Spain's best-known artists. (p114)

Plaza de Toros & Museo Taurino Visits to the bullring and its museum, though you pay for tours and bullfights. (p120)

Museo de Historia Free journey through Madrid's past, complete with a Goya. (p128)

Best Sometimes-Free Places

Museo del Prado Free 6pm to 8pm Monday to Saturday, and 5pm to 7pm Sunday. (p86)

Museo Thyssen-Bornemisza Free Monday. (p92)

Centro de Arte Reina Sofía Free 1.30pm to 7pm Sunday, and 7pm to 9pm Monday and Wednesday to Saturday. (p96)

Real Academia de Bellas Artes de San Fernando Free on Wednesday. (p71)

Basílica de San Francisco El Grande Free during mass times. (Pictured above; p56)

Four Perfect Days

Day 1

MARK READ/LONELY PLANET ©

So many Madrid days begin in the **Plaza Mayor** (p36), or perhaps nearby with a breakfast of *chocolate con churros* (pictured above) at **Chocolatería de San Ginés** (p46). While you're in the old town, drop by the **Plaza de la Villa** (p42) and **Plaza de Oriente** (p43).

Stop for a coffee or wine at **Cafe de Oriente** (p47), visit the **Palacio Real** (p38), then graze on tapas for lunch at the **Mercado de San Miguel** (p44). If you've only time to visit one Madrid art gallery, make it the **Museo del Prado** (p86), where you could easily spend an entire afternoon.

Dinner at **Restaurante Sobrino de Botín** (p83) is a fine way to spend your evening. Perhaps take in a flamenco show at **Las Tablas** (p47), followed by a cocktail at **Museo Chicote** (p131).

Day 2

KRZYSZTOF DYDYNSKI/LONELY PLANET ©

Get to the **Centro de Arte Reina Sofía** (p96) early to beat the crowds, then climb up through sedate streets to spend a couple of hours soaking up the calm of the **Parque del Buen Retiro** (pictured above; p100).

Wander down to admire the **Plaza de la Cibeles** (p103), have another tapas lunch at **Estado Puro** (p104) or **Los Gatos** (p75), then catch the metro across town to admire the Goya frescoes in the **Ermita de San Antonio de la Florida** (p138). Back in town, shop for souvenirs at **Casa de Diego** (p80), **El Arco Artesanía** (p48) and **Antigua Casa Talavera** (p48).

Check out if there's live jazz on offer at **Café Central** (p78), then have an after-show drink at **El Imperfecto** (p76) and dinner at **Casa Alberto** (p74).

Day 3

Spend the morning at the **Museo Thyssen-Bornemisza** (p92), then head out east to take a tour of the **Plaza de Toros** bullring (pictured above; p120), before spending the rest of the morning shopping along **Calle de Serrano**.

If you're feeling extravagant, try the thrilling experience of **Platea** (p115); if you've fallen in love with the idea of tapas, lunch instead at **Biotza** (p116). After lunch, spend an hour or two at the **Museo Lázaro Galdiano** (p108).

As dusk approaches, catch the metro across town to La Latina and spend as long as you can picking your way through the tapas bars of Calle de la Cava Baja. A wine at **Taberna El Tempranillo** (p60) and a mojito out on Plaza de la Paja at **Delic** (p60) should set you up for the night ahead.

Day 4

If you love art, an hour or two at **Real Academia de Bellas Artes de San Fernando** (p71) will nicely round out your experience of Madrid's art scene. It's also worth exploring the laneways of Malasaña between Calle de Pez, Plaza Dos de Mayo and the Glorieta de Bilbao.

Lunch at **Albur** (p130) or **Bazaar** (p129). If you've left a minimum of three hours to play with, take a train out of town to **Real Monasterio de San Lorenzo** (pictured above; p140) to enjoy the lavish palace-monastery complex.

Back in town, if you've calculated your run well, there's time for one last performance, this time at **Teatro de la Zarzuela** (p78). To round out your visit, hit **Almonte** (p117) or **El Junco Jazz Club** (p135), depending on what sort of memories you'd like to leave Madrid with.

Need to Know

For detailed information, see Survival Guide p145

Currency
Euro (€)

Language
Spanish (Castellano)

Visas
Generally not required for stays of up to 90 days (not at all for members of EU or Schengen countries). Some nationalities need a Schengen visa.

Money
ATMs are widely available. Credit cards are accepted in most hotels, restaurants and shops.

Mobile Phones
Local SIM cards are widely available and can be used in European and Australian mobile phones. Other phones may need to be set to roaming.

Time
Western European (GMT/UTC plus one hour during winter, plus two hours during daylight-saving period)

Tipping
Tipping is not common.

Daily Budget

Budget: Less than €100

Dorm bed: €15–25;

Hostal (budget hotel) double: €50–70

Three-course *menú del día* (daily set menu) lunches: €10–15

Sightseeing during free admission times

Midrange: €100–200

Double room in midrange hotel: €71–150

Lunch and/or dinner in decent restaurants: €20–50 per person per meal

Museum entry: €10–15

Top end: More than €200

Double room in top-end hotel: from €150

Fine dining for lunch and dinner: from €50 per person per meal

Cocktails: €8–15

Advance Planning

Three months before Book dinner at DiverXo (p11), Viridiana (p104), or La Terraza del Casino (p75).

One month before Book your accommodation, especially at the top end of the market.

One week before Book online entry to the Museo del Prado (p86) and tickets to a **Real Madrid game** (📞902 324 324; www.real madrid.com; Av de Concha Espina 1; tickets from €40; Ⓜ Santiago Bernabéu).

Arriving in Madrid

✈ Aeropuerto de Barajas (Adolfo Suárez Madrid-Barajas Airport)

Metro (6.05am to 1.30am), bus (€5) and minibus (both 24 hours) to central Madrid; taxis €30.

🚇 Estación de Atocha (Atocha Train Station)

Metro and bus to central Madrid (6.05am to 1.30am); taxi from €8.

🚇 Estación de Chamartín (Chamartín Train Station)

Metro and bus to central Madrid (6.05am to 1.30am); taxi around €13.

🚇 Estación Sur de Autobuses (Bus Station)

Metro and bus to central Madrid (6.05am to 1.30am); taxi from around €13.

Getting Around

Ten-trip Metrobús tickets cost €12.20, charged to your Tarjeta Multi, are valid for journeys on Madrid's metro and bus network. Tickets can be bought from most newspaper kiosks and *estancos* (tobacconists), as well as in staffed booths and ticket machines.

🚌 Bus

Visit www.emtmadrid.es for route maps and numbers.

Ⓜ Metro

Twelve colour-coded metro lines criss-cross central Madrid (www.metromadrid.es), although only numbers 1 to 10 are likely to be of use to travellers.

🚆 Train

The short-range *cercanías* (regional trains operated by Renfe) are handy for making a quick, north–south hop between Chamartín and Atocha train stations.

Madrid Neighbourhoods

Plaza Mayor & Royal Madrid (p35)

The heart of old Madrid with the city's grandest medieval architecture and fabulous places to eat and shop.

La Latina & Lavapiés (p51)

Medieval Madrid comes to life with some of Spain's best tapas and the iconic El Rastro market on Sunday mornings.

Ermita de San Antonio de la Florida

Palacio Real

Plaza Mayor

Sol, Santa Ana & Huertas (p67)

The city's beating heart, with relentless nightlife, live music, bars and restaurants to go with some of Madrid's prettiest streetscapes.

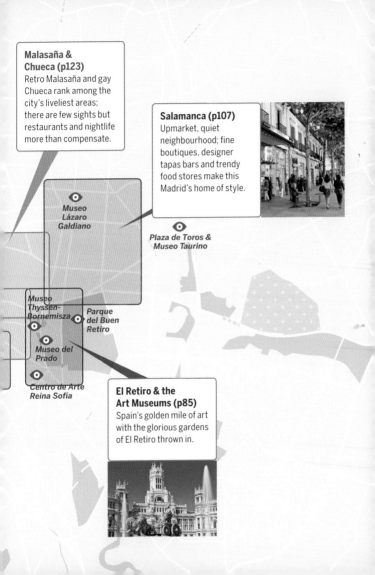

Malasaña & Chueca (p123)

Retro Malasaña and gay Chueca rank among the city's liveliest areas; there are few sights but restaurants and nightlife more than compensate.

Salamanca (p107)

Upmarket, quiet neighbourhood; fine boutiques, designer tapas bars and trendy food stores make this Madrid's home of style.

◉ Museo Lázaro Galdiano

◉ Plaza de Toros & Museo Taurino

Museo Thyssen-Bornemisza ◉

◉ Parque del Buen Retiro

◉ Museo del Prado

◉ Centro de Arte Reina Sofía

El Retiro & the Art Museums (p85)

Spain's golden mile of art with the glorious gardens of El Retiro thrown in.

Explore
Madrid

Worth a Trip 🔭

Madrid's Walking Tours 🥾

Monument to Alfonso XII, Parque del Buen Retiro (p100)

Explore ◈

Plaza Mayor & Royal Madrid

The bustling, compact and medieval heart of the city is where Madrid's story began and where the city became the seat of royal power. It's also where the splendour of imperial Spain was at its most ostentatious, with palaces, ancient churches, elegant squares and imposing convents. It's an architectural high point of the city, with plenty of fine eating and shopping options thrown in for good measure.

Plaza Mayor is the hub of Madrid's most medieval quarter, an area known as Madrid de los Austrias, in reference to the Habsburg dynasty, which ruled Spain from 1517 to 1700. The plaza is a place both to admire and to get your bearings, the place where so many explorations of the neighbourhood (and wider city) begin. That's because it is at once the hub of neighbourhood life and the topographical high point of the barrio (district).

The neighbourhood's shops, restaurants, bars and nightclubs tend to be concentrated at the eastern end, close to Plaza Mayor, while the architectural highlights are more evenly spread.

Getting There

M A short step from Plaza Mayor, Sol metro station is one of the most useful in Madrid, with lines 1, 2 and 3 all passing through. Ópera (lines 2 and 5) is another useful neighbourhood station – line 2 can carry you to the Paseo del Prado (leaving a short walk to the galleries), Parque del Buen Retiro or Salamanca in no time.

Neighbourhood Map on p40

Catedral de Nuestra Señora de la Almudena, Palacio Real (p38)
EMPERORCOSAR/SHUTTERSTOCK ©

Top Sight 📷
Plaza Mayor

*It's easy to fall in love with Madrid in the Plaza
Mayor. This is the monumental heart of the city
and the grand stage for so many of its most
important historical events. Here, Madrid's
relentless energy courses across its cobblestones
beneath ochre-hued apartments, wrought-iron
balconies, frescoes and stately spires.*

◉ MAP P40, E6

Ⓜ Sol

History's Tale

Designed in 1619 by Juan Gómez de Mora and built in typical Herrerian style, of which the slate spires are the most obvious expression, Plaza Mayor's first public ceremony was the beatification of San Isidro Labrador (St Isidro the Farm Labourer), Madrid's patron saint. Bullfights, often in celebration of royal weddings or births, with royalty watching on from the balconies and up to 50,000 people crammed into the plaza, were a recurring theme until 1878. Far more notorious were the autos-da-fé (the ritual condemnations of heretics during the Spanish Inquisition) followed by executions – burnings at the stake and deaths by garrotte on the north side of the square, hangings to the south.

Real Casa de la Panadería

The exquisite frescoes of the 17th-century **Real Casa de la Panadería** (Royal Bakery; Plaza Mayor 27) rank among Madrid's more eye-catching sights. The present frescoes date to just 1992 and are the work of artist Carlos Franco, who chose images from the signs of the zodiac and gods (eg Cybele) to provide a stunning backdrop for the plaza. The frescoes were inaugurated to coincide with Madrid's 1992 spell as European Capital of Culture. The building now houses the city's main tourist office.

Felipe III

In the middle of the square stands an equestrian statue of the man who ordered the plaza's construction: Felipe III. Originally placed in the Casa de Campo, it was moved to Plaza Mayor in 1848, whereafter it became a favoured meeting place for irreverent *madrileños* (people from Madrid), who arranged to catch up 'under the balls of the horse'.

★ Top Tips

o To see the plaza's epic history told in pictures, check out the carvings on the circular seats beneath the lamp posts (and growing number of padlocks).

o On Sunday mornings, the plaza's arcaded perimeter is taken over by traders of old coins, banknotes and stamps.

o In December and early January the plaza is occupied by a popular Christmas market selling the season's kitsch.

o The bars and restaurants with outdoor tables spilling onto the plaza are often overpriced and best avoided.

✗ Take a Break

Just beyond the square's western perimeter, the Mercado de San Miguel (p44) combines historical architecture with one of Madrid's most exciting eating experiences.

For fast food Madrid style, try a *bocadillo de calamares* (a roll filled with deep-fried calamari) at La Ideal (p44).

Top Sight 📷
Palacio Real

You can almost imagine how the eyes of Felipe V, the first of the Bourbon kings, lit up when the alcázar (Muslim-era fortress) burned down in 1734 on Madrid's most exclusive patch of real estate. His plan? Build a palace that would dwarf all its European counterparts. The resulting 2800-room royal palace never attained such a scale, but it's still an Italianate baroque architectural landmark of arresting beauty.

◎ **MAP P40, B6**

www.patrimonio
nacional.es

Calle de Bailén

adult/concession €11/6,
guide/audioguide €4/3,
EU citizens free last 2hr
Mon-Thu

🕐10am-8pm Apr-Sep, to
6pm Oct-Mar

Ⓜ Ópera

Plaza de la Armería

The Plaza de la Armería (Plaza de Armas; Plaza of the Armoury) courtyard puts the sheer scale of the palace into perspective, and it's from here that Madrid's cathedral (Catedral de Nuestra Señora de la Almudena) takes on its most pleasing aspect. The colourful changing of the guard in full parade dress takes place at noon on the first Wednesday of every month (except August and September) between the palace and the cathedral, with a less extravagant changing of the guard inside the palace compound at the Puerta del Príncipe every Wednesday from 11am to 2pm.

Salón del Trono

From the northern end of the Plaza de la Armería, the main stairway, a grand statement of imperial power, leads to the royal apartments and eventually to the Salón del Trono (Throne Room). The room is nauseatingly lavish with its crimson-velvet wall coverings complemented by a ceiling painted by the dramatic Venetian baroque master, Tiepolo.

Gasparini & Porcelana

Close to the Throne Room, the Salón de Gasparini (Gasparini Room) has an exquisite stucco ceiling and walls resplendent with embroidered silks. The aesthetic may be different in the Sala de Porcelana (Porcelain Room), but the aura of extravagance continues with myriad pieces from the one-time Retiro porcelain factory screwed into the walls.

Jardines de Sabatini

The French-inspired **Jardines de Sabatini** (admission free; 🕑9am-10pm May-Sep, to 9pm Oct-Apr; Ⓜ Ópera) lie along the northern flank of the Palacio Real. They were laid out in the 1930s to replace the royal stables that once stood on the site. These quite formal gardens with fountains and small labyrinths offer a fine alternative view of the palace's northern facade.

★ Top Tips

○ Plan to get here at 10am before the tour buses start to arrive.

○ Have a Plan B in case there's a royal event that closes the palace on the day you wish to visit.

○ A guided tour or audioguide will greatly enhance your experience of the palace.

✕ Take a Break

There's no finer perch in Madrid than the outdoor tables of Cafe de Oriente (p47) that look out towards the palace.

El Café de la Opera (🕿 91 542 63 82; www.elcafedelaopera.com; Calle de Arrieta 6; 🕑8am-midnight; 🛜; Ⓜ Ópera) across the road from Madrid's opera house, has a refined air and live opera in the evenings.

Plaza Mayor & Royal Madrid

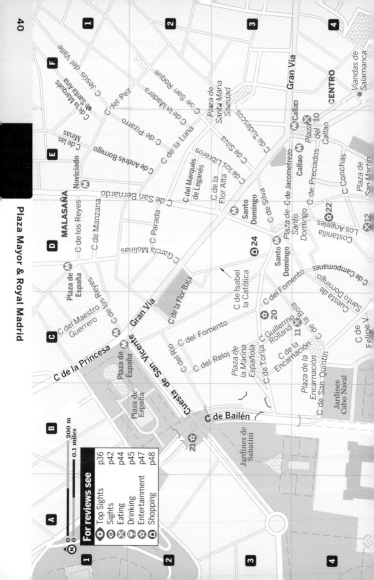

For reviews see

◎ Top Sights	p36
◉ Sights	p42
✗ Eating	p44
✗ Drinking	p45
✪ Entertainment	p47
⛭ Shopping	p48

200 m
0.1 miles

CENTRO

MALASAÑA

Plaza de España

Gran Via

C de la Princesa

Cuesta de San Vicente

C de Bailén

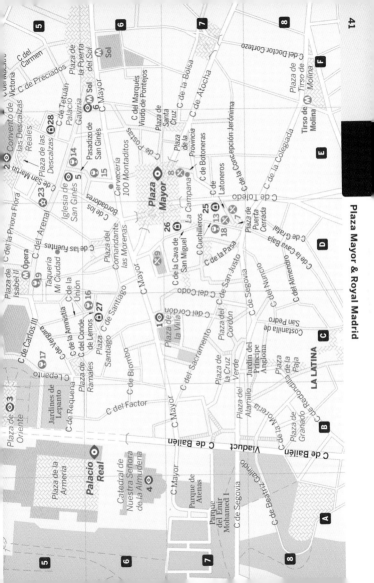

Plaza Mayor & Royal Madrid

41

Sights

Plaza de la Villa

SQUARE

1 ⦿ MAP P40, C6

The intimate Plaza de la Villa is one of Madrid's prettiest. Enclosed on three sides by wonderfully preserved examples of 17th-century *barroco madrileño* (Madrid-style baroque architecture – a pleasing amalgam of brick, exposed stone and wrought iron), it was the permanent seat of Madrid's city government from the Middle Ages until recent years, when Madrid's city council relocated to the grand Palacio de Cibeles on Plaza de la Cibeles (p103).

On the western side of the square is the 17th-century **former town hall**, in Habsburg-style baroque with Herrerian slate-tile spires. On the opposite side of the square is the Gothic **Casa de los Lujanes**, whose brickwork tower is said to have been 'home' to the imprisoned French monarch François I after his capture in the Battle of Pavia (1525). Legend has it that as the star prisoner was paraded down Calle Mayor, locals are said to have been more impressed by the splendidly attired Frenchman than they were by his more drab captor, the Spanish Habsburg emperor Carlos I, much to the chagrin of the latter. The plateresque (15th- and 16th-century Spanish baroque) **Casa de Cisneros**, built in 1537 with later Renaissance alterations, also catches the eye. (Ⓜ Ópera)

Cathedral Extras

Climb up through the Museo de la Catedral y Cúpola of the Catedral de Nuestra Señora de la Almudena on the northern facade, opposite the Palacio Real, for fine views from the top. Down the hill beneath the cathedral's southern wall on Calle Mayor is a neo-Romanesque crypt, with more than 400 columns, 20 chapels and fine stained-glass windows.

Convento de las Descalzas Reales

CONVENT

2 ⦿ MAP P40, E5

The grim plateresque walls of the Convento de las Descalzas Reales offer no hint that behind the facade lies a sumptuous stronghold of the faith. The compulsory guided tour (in Spanish) leads you up a gaudily frescoed Renaissance stairway to the upper level of the cloister. The vault was painted by Claudio Coello, one of the most important artists of the Madrid School of the 17th century and whose works adorn San Lorenzo de El Escorial. (Convent of the Barefoot Royals; www.patrimonio nacional.es; Plaza de las Descalzas 3; €6, incl Convento de la Encarnación €8; 🕙10am-2pm & 4-6.30pm Tue-Sat, 10am-3pm Sun; Ⓜ Ópera, Sol)

Plaza de Oriente

SQUARE

3 ⊙ MAP P40, B5

A royal palace that once had aspirations to be the Spanish Versailles. Sophisticated cafes watched over by apartments that cost the equivalent of a royal salary. The **Teatro Real** (📞902 244848; www.teatro-real.com), Madrid's opera house and one of Spain's temples to high culture. Some of the finest sunset views in Madrid... Welcome to Plaza de Oriente, a living, breathing monument to imperial Madrid. (ⓂÓpera)

Catedral de Nuestra Señora de la Almudena

CATHEDRAL

4 ⊙ MAP P40, A6

Paris has Notre Dame and Rome has St Peter's Basilica. In fact, almost every European city of stature has its signature cathedral, a standout monument to a glorious Christian past. Not Madrid. Although the exterior of this cathedral sits in harmony with the adjacent Palacio Real, Madrid's cathedral is cavernous and largely charmless within; its colourful, modern ceilings do little to make up for the lack of old-world gravitas that so distinguishes great cathedrals. (📞91 542 22 00; www.catedraldelaalmudena.es; Calle de Bailén; cathedral & crypt by donation, museum adult/child €6/4; ⊙9am-8.30pm Mon-Sat, museum 10am-2.30pm Mon-Sat; ⓂÓpera)

Iglesia de San Ginés

CHURCH

5 ⊙ MAP P40, E5

Due north of Plaza Mayor, San Ginés is one of Madrid's oldest churches: it has been here in one form or another since at least the 14th century. What you see today was built in 1645 but largely reconstructed after a fire in 1824. The church houses some fine paintings, including El Greco's *Expulsion of the Moneychangers from the Temple* (1614), which is beautifully displayed; the glass is just 6mm from the canvas to avoid reflections. (Calle del Arenal 13; admission free; ⊙8.45am-1pm & 6-9pm Mon-Sat, 9.45am-2pm & 6-9pm Sun; ⓂSol, Ópera)

Palacio Gaviria

MUSEUM

6 ⊙ MAP P40, F6

Until recently this 19th-century Italianate palace was a nightclub. It has been artfully converted to a dynamic artistic space, with major temporary art exhibitions that have included an Escher retrospective and the works of Alphonse Mucha. Coupled with high-quality exhibitions is a soaring Renaissance palace with extraordinary ceiling frescoes. Put all of this together and you've one of the more exciting additions to Madrid's artistic portfolio. (📞902 044226; Calle del Arenal 9; adult/child €12/free; ⊙10am-8pm Sun-Thu, to 9pm Fri & Sat; ⓂSol)

Eating

Casa Revuelta

TAPAS €

7 ❌ MAP P40, D7

Casa Revuelta puts out some of Madrid's finest tapas of bacalao (cod) bar none – unlike elsewhere, *tajadas de bacalao* don't have bones in them and slide down the throat with the greatest of ease. Early on a Sunday afternoon, as the Rastro crowd gathers here, it's filled to the rafters. Other specialities include *torreznos* (bacon bits), *callos* (tripe), and *albóndigas* (meatballs). (📞91 366 33 32; Calle de Latoneros 3; tapas from €3; ⏱10.30am-4pm & 7-11pm Tue-Sat, 10.30am-4pm Sun, closed Aug; Ⓜ Sol, La Latina)

La Ideal

SPANISH €

8 ❌ MAP P40, E7

Spanish bars don't come any more basic than this, but it's the purveyor of that enduring and wildly popular Madrid tradition – the *bocadillo de calamares*. If it's closed, which is rare, plenty of bars elsewhere around the plaza offer the same deal. (📞91 365 72 78; Calle de Botoneras 4; bocadillos from €2.90; ⏱9am-11pm Sun-Thu, to midnight Fri & Sat; Ⓜ Sol)

Mercado de San Miguel

TAPAS €

9 ❌ MAP P40, D6

This is one of Madrid's oldest and most beautiful markets, within early-20th-century glass walls and an inviting space strewn with tables. You can order tapas and sometimes more substantial plates at most of the counter-bars, and everything here (from caviar to chocolate) is as tempting as the market is alive. Put simply, it's one of our favourite experiences in Madrid. (📞91 542 49 36; www.mercadodesanmiguel.es; Plaza de San Miguel; tapas from €1.50; ⏱10am-midnight Sun-Wed, to 2am Thu-Sat; Ⓜ Sol)

Gourmet Experience

FOOD HALL €€

10 ❌ MAP P40, E4

Ride the elevator up to the 9th floor of the El Corte Inglés department store for one of downtown Madrid's best eating experiences. The food is excellent, with everything from top-notch tapas or sushi to gourmet hamburgers, and the views fabulous, especially those

Calamari Roll

🍽

One of the lesser-known culinary specialities of Madrid is a *bocadillo de calamares* (a small baguette-style roll filled to bursting with deep-fried calamari). You'll find them in many bars in the streets surrounding Plaza Mayor and neighbouring bars along Calle de los Botaneros, off Plaza Mayor's southeastern corner. Try La Ideal. At around €2.90, it's the perfect street snack.

Local Specialities

In addition to the chickpea-and-meat hotpot that is *cocido a la madrileña*, Taberna La Bola serves up other Madrid specialities such as callos (tripe) and sopa castellana (garlic soup).

that look over Plaza del Callao and down Gran Vía. (www.elcorteingles.es; 9th fl, Plaza del Callao 2; mains €8-20; ⏱10am-10pm; Ⓜ Callao)

Taberna La Bola   SPANISH €€

11 ⊗ MAP P40, C4

Going strong since 1870 and run by the sixth generation of the Verdasco family, Taberna La Bola is a much-loved bastion of traditional Madrid cuisine. If you're going to try *cocido a la madrileña* while in Madrid, this is a good place to do so. It's busy and noisy and very Madrid. (☏ 91 547 69 30; www.labola.es; Calle de la Bola 5; mains €8-25; ⏱1.30-4.30pm & 8.30-11pm Mon-Sat, 1.30-4.30pm Sun, closed Aug; Ⓜ Santo Domingo)

El Pato Mudo   SPANISH €€

12 ⊗ MAP P40, D4

El Pato Mudo isn't the most famous paella restaurant in Madrid, but it's known to locals for its variety of outstanding rice dishes at reasonable prices. Specialities include black rice with squid ink, soupy rice, authentic *paella valenciana* and shellfish paella.

Served directly from the pan for two or more people, they go well with the local wines. (☏ 91 559 48 40; elpatomudo@hotmail.es; Calle Costanilla de los Ángeles 8; mains €13-24; ⏱1-4pm & 8-11.30pm Wed-Sun; Ⓜ Ópera)

Restaurante Sobrino de Botín   CASTILIAN €€€

13 ⊗ MAP P40, D7

It's not every day that you can eat in the oldest restaurant in the world (as recognised by the *Guinness Book of Records* – established in 1725). The secret of its staying power is fine *cochinillo asado* (roast suckling pig) and *cordero asado* (roast lamb) cooked in wood-fired ovens. Eating in the vaulted cellar is a treat. (☏ 91 366 42 17; www.botin.es; Calle de los Cuchilleros 17; mains €18-27; ⏱1-4pm & 8pm-midnight; Ⓜ La Latina, Sol)

Drinking

Teatro Joy Eslava   CLUB

14 ⊕ MAP P40, E5

The only things guaranteed at this grand old Madrid dance club (housed in a 19th-century theatre) are a crowd and the fact that it'll be open (it claims to have operated every single day since 1981). The music and the people are a mixed bag, but queues are long and invariably include locals, tourists, and the occasional *famoso* (celebrity). (Joy Madrid; ☏ 91 366 37 33; www.joy-eslava.com; Calle del Arenal 11; admission €12-15; ⏱11.30pm-6am; Ⓜ Sol)

Between Meals & Spanish Fast Food

If you're still adjusting to Spanish restaurant hours and need a meal in between, there are a number of options in the centre.

When it comes to local fast food, one of the lesser known culinary specialities of Madrid is a *bocadillo de calamares* (a small baguette-style roll filled to bursting with deep-fried calamari). You'll find them in many bars in the streets surrounding Plaza Mayor and neighbouring bars along Calle de Botoneras off Plaza Mayor's southeastern corner. At around €2.70, it's the perfect street snack. Try the following for between-meal snacks.

Mercado de San Miguel (p44) All-day tapas.

Taquería Mi Ciudad (Map p40, D5; ☎ 608 621 096; www.taqueria miciudad.com; Calle de las Fuentes 11; tacos €1.50; ⏱11am-1.30am; Ⓜ Ópera) Budget tacos.

La Campana (Map p40, E7; ☎ 91 364 29 84; Calle de Botoneras 6; bocadillos from €2.90; ⏱9am-11pm Sun-Thu, to midnight Fri & Sat; Ⓜ Sol) *Bocadillos de calamares.*

La Ideal (p44) *Bocadillos de calamares.*

Viandas de Salamanca (Map p40, F4; ☎ 91 521 27 74; www.viandas desalamanca.es; Calle del Carmen 27; bocadillos €4; ⏱10.30am-10.30pm Sun-Thu, to 11pm Fri & Sat; Ⓜ Callao, Sol) *Jamón* rolls.

Cervecería 100 Montaditos (Map p40, E6; www.spain.100 montaditos.com; Calle Mayor 22; montaditos €1-3; ⏱noon-midnight; Ⓜ Sol) Tiny *bocadillos.*

Chocolatería de San Ginés

CAFE

15 🍴 MAP P40, E6

One of the grand icons of the Madrid night, this *chocolate con churros* cafe sees a sprinkling of tourists throughout the day, but locals pack it out in their search for sustenance on their way home from a nightclub somewhere close to dawn. Only in Madrid... (☎ 91 365 65 46; www.chocolateriasangines. com; Pasadizo de San Ginés 5; ⏱24hr; Ⓜ Sol)

Anticafé

CAFE

16 🍴 MAP P40, C6

Bohemian kitsch at its best is the prevailing theme here and it runs right through the decor and regular cultural events (poetry readings and concerts). As such, it won't be to everyone's taste, but we think it adds some much-needed variety to the downtown drinking scene. (www.anticafe.es; Calle de la Unión 2; ⏱5pm-2am Tue-Sun; Ⓜ Ópera)

Cafe de Oriente
CAFE

17 MAP P40, C5

The outdoor tables of this distinguished old cafe are among the most sought-after in central Madrid, providing as they do a front-row seat for the beautiful Plaza de Oriente, with the Palacio Real as a backdrop. The building itself was once part of a long-gone, 17th-century convent and the interior feels a little like a set out of Mitteleuropa. (☏91 541 39 74; Plaza de Oriente 2; ⏱8.30am-1.30am Mon-Thu, 9am-2.30am Fri & Sat, 9am-1.30am Sun; MÓpera)

Bodegas Ricla
BAR

18 MAP P40, D7

This bar is so tiny you might be rubbing haunches with other customers as you sip your wine. For more than 100 years, it's been serving tasty authentic tapas and local vintages: red, white and pink wines, *cavas* and vermouth. Inside, little has changed in decades, with old-style terracotta barrels and pictures of bullfighters lining the walls. (☏91 365 20 69; Calle Cuchilleros 6; ⏱1-4pm & 7pm-midnight Wed-Sat & Mon, 1-4pm Sun; MTirso de Molina)

Café del Real
BAR

19 MAP P40, D5

A cafe and cocktail bar in equal parts, this intimate little place serves up creative coffees and a few cocktails (the mojitos are excellent) to the soundtrack of chill-out music. The best seats are upstairs, where the low ceilings, wooden beams and leather chairs make for a great place to pass an afternoon with friends. (☏91 547 21 24; Plaza de Isabel II 2; ⏱8am-1am Mon-Thu, to 2.30am Fri, 9am-2.30am Sat, 10am-11.30pm Sun; MÓpera)

Entertainment

Café de Chinitas
FLAMENCO

20 MAP P40, C3

One of the most distinguished *tablaos* (flamenco venues) in Madrid, drawing in everyone from the Spanish royal family to Bill Clinton, Café de Chinitas has an elegant setting and top-notch performers. It may attract loads of tourists, but its authentic flamenco also gives it top marks. Reservations are highly recommended. (☏91 547 15 02; www.chinitas.com; Calle de Torija 7; admission incl drink/meal €36/55; ⏱shows 8.15pm & 10.30pm Mon-Sat; MSanto Domingo)

Las Tablas
FLAMENCO

21 MAP P40, B2

Las Tablas has a reputation for quality flamenco and reasonable prices; it's among the best choices in town. Most nights you'll see a classic flamenco show, with plenty of throaty singing and soul-baring dancing. Antonia Moya and Marisol Navarro, leading lights in the flamenco world, are regular performers here. (☏91 542 05 20; www.lastablasmadrid.com; Plaza de España 9; admission incl drink from €29; ⏱shows 8pm & 10pm; MPlaza de España)

Café Berlin
JAZZ

22 ⭐ MAP P40, D4

El Berlín has been something of a Madrid jazz stalwart since the 1950s, although a makeover has brought flamenco (Wednesday is a flamenco jam session), R&B, soul, funk and fusion into the mix. Headline acts play at 11pm, although check the website as some can begin as early as 9pm. (☎ 91 559 74 29; www.berlincafe.es; Costanilla de los Ángeles 20; €5-20; ⏰ 9pm-3am Tue-Thu, to 5am Fri & Sat; Ⓜ Santo Domingo)

La Coquette Blues
LIVE MUSIC

23 ⭐ MAP P40, E5

Madrid's best blues bar has been around since the 1980s and its 8pm Sunday jam session is legendary. Live acts perform Tuesday to Thursday at 10.30pm and the atmosphere is very cool at any time. (☎ 91 530 80 95; Calle de las Hileras 14; ⏰ 8pm-3am Tue-Thu, to 3.30am Fri & Sat, 7pm-3am Sun; Ⓜ Ópera)

Shopping

Antigua Casa Talavera
CERAMICS

24 🔒 MAP P40, D3

The extraordinary tiled facade of this wonderful old shop conceals an Aladdin's cave of ceramics from all over Spain. This is not the mass-produced stuff aimed at a tourist market, but instead comes from the small family potters of Andalucía and Toledo, ranging from the decorative (tiles) to the useful (plates, jugs and other kitchen items). The elderly couple who run the place are delightful. (☎ 91 547 34 17; www.antiguacasatalavera.com; Calle de Isabel la Católica 2; ⏰ 10am-1.30pm & 5-8pm Mon-Fri, 10am-1.30pm Sat; Ⓜ Santo Domingo)

Casa Hernanz
SHOES

25 🔒 MAP P40, D7

Comfy, rope-soled *alpargatas* (espadrilles), Spain's traditional summer footwear, are worn by everyone from the king of Spain down. You can buy your own pair at this humble workshop, which has been handmaking the shoes for five generations; you can even get them made to order. Prices range from €6 to €40 and queues form whenever the weather starts to warm up. (☎ 91 366 54 50; www.alpargateriahernanz.com; Calle de Toledo 18; ⏰ 9am-1.30pm & 4.30-8pm Mon-Fri, 10am-2pm Sat; Ⓜ La Latina, Sol)

El Arco Artesanía
ARTS & CRAFTS

26 🔒 MAP P40, D7

This original shop in the southwestern corner of Plaza Mayor sells an outstanding array of homemade designer souvenirs, from stone, ceramic and glass work to jewellery and home fittings. The papier-mâché figures are gorgeous, but there's so much else here to turn your head. It sometimes closes earlier in the depths of winter. (☎ 91 365 26 80;

Chocolatería de San Ginés (p46)

www.artesaniaelarco.com; Plaza Mayor 9; ⊘11am-10pm; Ⓜ Sol, La Latina)

El Flamenco Vive   FLAMENCO

27 🔒 MAP P40, C6

This temple to flamenco has it all, from guitars and songbooks to well-priced CDs, polka-dotted dancing costumes, shoes, colourful plastic jewellery and literature about flamenco. It's the sort of place that will appeal as much to curious first-timers as to serious students of the art. It also organises classes in flamenco guitar. (📞91 547 39 17; www.elflamencovive. es; Calle Conde de Lemos 7; ⊘10am-2pm & 5-8.30pm Mon-Fri, 10am-2pm Sat; Ⓜ Ópera)

Maty   FLAMENCO

28 🔒 MAP P40, E5

Wandering around central Madrid, it's easy to imagine that flamenco outfits have been reduced to imitation dresses sold as souvenirs to tourists. That's why places like Maty matter. Here you'll find dresses, shoes and all the accessories that go with the genre, with sizes for children and adults. These are the real deal, with prices to match, but they make brilliant gifts. (📞91 531 32 91; www.maty.es; Calle del Maestro Victoria 2; ⊘10am-1.45pm & 4.30-8pm Mon-Fri, 10am-2pm & 4.30-8pm Sat, 11am-2.30pm & 4.30-8pm 1st Sun of month; Ⓜ Sol)

Explore ⊛

La Latina & Lavapiés

La Latina combines Madrid's best selection of tapas bars, fine little boutiques and a medieval streetscape studded with elegant churches; graceful Calle de la Cava Baja could be our favourite street for tapas in town. Down the hill, Lavapiés is one of the city's oldest barrios (districts) and the heart of multicultural Madrid. Spanning the two neighbourhoods is the Sunday flea market of El Rastro.

La Latina's proximity to Plaza Mayor and the downtown area make it an easy area to dip into. Need a break nursing a mojito on a warm afternoon? Head for Plaza de la Paja and linger for as much time as you can spare. Eager to understand the buzz surrounding tapas and the local passion for going on a tapas crawl? Most evenings of the week are busy along Calle de la Cava Baja, but early Sunday lunchtime when the El Rastro crowds pour into La Latina is when you'll most appreciate being here.

With few sights to speak of, Lavapiés is a good place for an afternoon stroll or an evening spent catching the sights and sounds of Madrid's most multicultural corner.

Getting There

Ⓜ Unless you're walking from Plaza Mayor (an easy, agreeable stroll), La Latina metro station (line 5) is the best metro station both for the tapas bars of La Latina and El Rastro; Tirso de Molina station (line 1) is also OK. If you're only visiting Lavapiés or don't mind a steep uphill climb to La Latina, Lavapiés station (line 3) is your best bet.

Neighbourhood Map on p54

Walking Tour 🥾

El Rastro Sunday

There are few more enduring Madrid traditions than visiting El Rastro, believed to be Europe's largest flea market, on a Sunday. But El Rastro is so much more than a market: it's the prelude to an afternoon of vermouth and tapas in the bars of La Latina. Join the eating and drinking throngs, and you'll fulfil a key criteria of being considered a local.

Walk Facts

Start El Rastro; Ⓜ La Latina

End Delic; Ⓜ La Latina

Length 2km; two to three hours

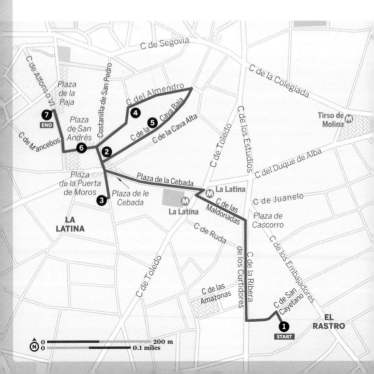

❶ El Rastro

You could easily spend a Sunday morning inching your way down the Calle de la Ribera de los Curtidores, the street that hosts **El Rastro** (Calle de la Ribera de los Curtidores; ⏰8am-3pm Sun). Cheap clothes, old flamenco records, even older photos of Madrid, faux designer purses, grungy T-shirts and household goods are the main fare. For every 10 pieces of junk, there's a real gem (a lost masterpiece, an Underwood typewriter...).

❷ Vermouth Hour

Sunday. One o'clock in the afternoon. A busy bar along Calle de la Cava Baja. Welcome to *la hora del vermut* (vermouth hour), a longstanding Madrid tradition whereby friends and families enjoy a post-Rastro aperitif. This tradition is deeply engrained in *madrileño* culture and most such bars are along or just off Calle de la Cava Baja.

❸ Txirimiri

Every local has a favourite place for ordering a *pincho de tortilla* (a *tapa* of *tortilla de patatas*, the quintessentially Spanish potato omelette). But food critics and your average punter alike are drawn in ever-increasing numbers to the Basque bar Txirimiri (p57).

❹ Almendro 13

Almendro 13 (p57) is a wildly popular *taberna* where you come for traditional Spanish tapas with an emphasis on quality rather than frilly elaborations. Cured meats, cheeses, omelettes and many variations on these themes dominate the menu; the famously good *huevos rotos* (literally, 'broken eggs') served with *jamón* (ham) and thin potato slices is the star.

❺ Casa Lucas

Casa Lucas (📞91 365 08 04; www.casalucas.es; Calle de la Cava Baja 30; tapas/raciones from €5/12; ⏰1-3.30pm & 8pm-midnight Thu-Tue, 1-3.30pm Wed) takes a sideways glance at traditional Spanish tapas, then heads off in new directions. There is a range of hot and cold tapas and larger *raciones*. The menu changes regularly as the chef comes up with new ideas, and particular attention is paid to the wine list.

❻ Plaza de San Andrés

While half of Madrid filters out across the city, either heading home or to the Parque del Buen Retiro, the remainder hang out in the Plaza de San Andrés, with its storeys-high mural and fine church backdrop. As the sun nears the horizon, the light softens and the gathered hordes start the drumbeats and begin to dance.

❼ Delic

We could go on for hours about Delic (p60), a longstanding cafe-bar, but we'll reduce it to its most basic elements: nursing an exceptionally good mojito (€8) or three on a warm summer's evening at Delic's outdoor tables on one of Madrid's prettiest plazas is one of life's great pleasures. Bliss.

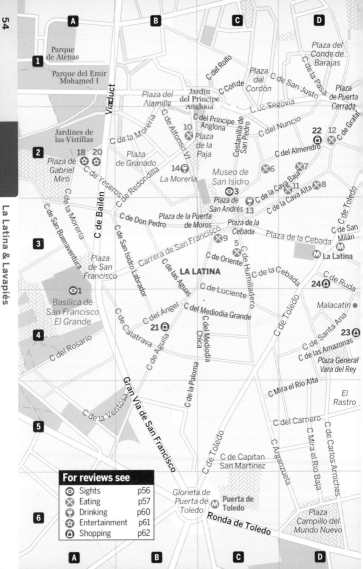

La Latina & Lavapiés

A **B** **C** **D**

1

Parque
de Atenas

Parque del Emir
Mohamed I

Viaduct

Plaza del Rollo

C del Conde

Plaza
del
Cordón

C de San Justo

C de la Pasa

Plaza del
Conde de
Barajas

C de Gratal

Plaza
de Puerta
Cerrada

Jardín
del Príncipe
Anglona

C de Segovia

Plaza del
Alamillo

C del Príncipe de
Anglona

C del Nuncio

2

Jardines de
las Vistillas

C de la Morería

C del Alfonso VI

10

Plaza
de la
Paja

Costanilla de
San Pedro

22 12

C del Almendro

18 20

Plaza de
Gabriel
Miró

C de Yeseros

Plaza
de Granado

14
La Morería

Museo de
San Isidro
3

6

C de la Cava Baja

7

11

8

C de la Cava Alta

C de Bailén

C de Redondilla

Plaza de
San Andrés

13

C de Toledo

3

C de la Morería

C de San Buenaventura

C de Don Pedro

Plaza de la Puerta
de Moros

Plaza de la
Cebada

Plaza de la Cebada

C de San
Milán

M La Latina

Plaza de
San
Francisco

C de San Isidro Labrador

Carrera de San Francisco

9

5

C de Oriente

C de Humilladero

C de Ruda

24

4

1
Basílica de
San Francisco
El Grande

C del Rosario

C de las Aguas

C de Calatrava

C del Ángel

21

LA LATINA

C de Luciente

C del Mediodía Grande

Malacatín

C de Santa Ana

23

C de las Amazonas

Plaza General
Vara del Rey

C de Toledo

5

C de la Ventosa

Gran Vía de San Francisco

C del Mediodía
Chica

C de la Paloma

C Mira el Río Alta

El
Rastro

C del Carnero

C Mira el Río Baja

C Arganzuela

C de Carlos Arniches

6

For reviews see	
◉ Sights	p56
🍴 Eating	p57
🍷 Drinking	p60
★ Entertainment	p61
🔒 Shopping	p62

C de Toledo

C de Capitán
San Martínez

Glorieta de
Puerta de
Toledo

M Puerta de
Toledo

Ronda de Toledo

Plaza
Campillo del
Mundo Nuevo

A **B** **C** **D**

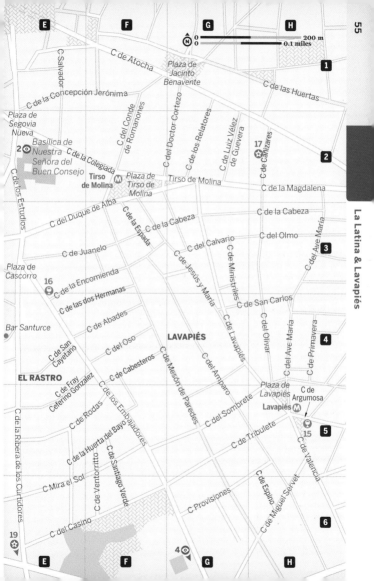

Sights

Basílica de San Francisco El Grande CHURCH

1 ⊙ MAP P54, A4

Lording it over the southwestern corner of La Latina, this imposing baroque basilica is one of Madrid's grandest old churches. Its extravagantly frescoed dome is, by some estimates, the largest in Spain and the fourth largest in the world, with a height of 56m and diameter of 33m. (Plaza de San Francisco 1; adult/concession €5/3; ⊙mass 8-10.30am Mon-Sat, museum 10.30am-12.30pm & 4-6pm Tue-Sun Sep-Jun, 10.30am-12.30pm & 5-7pm Tue-Sun Jul & Aug; Ⓜ La Latina, Puerta de Toledo)

San Francisco El Grande

Highlights include the neo-plateresque Capilla de San Bernardino (where the central fresco was painted by a young Goya), the museum (with works of art by Francisco Zurbarán and Francisco Pacheco, the father-in-law and teacher of Velázquez) and the fine Renaissance *sillería* (sculpted walnut seats) in the sacristy.

Although entry to the Basílica de San Francisco El Grande is free during morning Mass times, there is no access to the museum and the lights in the Capilla de San Bernardino won't be on to illuminate the Goya.

Basílica de Nuestra Señora del Buen Consejo CHURCH

2 ⊙ MAP P54, E2

Towering above the northern end of bustling Calle de Toledo, and visible through the arches from Plaza Mayor, this imposing church long served as the city's de facto cathedral until the Catedral de Nuestra Señora de la Almudena (p43) was completed in 1992. Still known to locals as the Catedral de San Isidro, the austere baroque basilica was founded in the 17th century as the headquarters for the Jesuits. (Catedral de San Isidro; ☎91 369 20 37; Calle de Toledo 37; ⊙7.30am-1pm & 6-9pm; Ⓜ Tirso de Molina, La Latina)

Museo de San Isidro MUSEUM

3 ⊙ MAP P54, C2

This engaging museum occupies the spot where San Isidro Labrador, patron saint of Madrid, ended his days in around 1172. A particular highlight is the large model based on Pedro Teixeira's famous 1656 map of Madrid. Of great historical interest (though not much to look at) is the 'miraculous well', where the saint called forth water to slake his master's thirst. In another miracle, the son of the saint's master fell into a well, whereupon Isidro prayed until the water rose and lifted his master's son to safety. (Museo de los Origenes; ☎91 366 74 15; www.madrid.es; Plaza de San Andrés 2; admission free; ⊙10am-7pm Tue-Sun mid-Jun–mid-Sep, 9.30am-8pm Tue-Sun rest of year; Ⓜ La Latina)

Matadero Madrid

ARTS CENTRE

4 📍 MAP P54, G6

This contemporary arts centre is a stunning multipurpose space south of the centre. Occupying the converted buildings of the old Arganzuela livestock market and slaughterhouse, Matadero Madrid covers 148,300 sq metres and hosts cutting-edge drama, musical and dance performances and exhibitions on architecture, fashion, literature and cinema. It's a dynamic space and its proximity to the landscaped riverbank makes for a nontouristy alternative to sightseeing in Madrid, not to mention a brilliant opportunity to see the latest avant-garde theatre or exhibitions. (📞91 252 52 53; www.mataderomadrid.com; Paseo de la Chopera 14; admission free; 🚇Legazpi)

Eating

Txirimiri

TAPAS €

5 🍴 MAP P54, C3

This *pintxos* (Basque tapas) bar is a great little discovery just down from the main La Latina tapas circuit. Wonderful wines, gorgeous *pinchos* (the *tortilla de patatas* – potato and onion omelette – is superb) and fine risottos add up to a pretty special combination. (📞91 364 11 96; www.txirimiri.es; Calle del Humilladero 6; tapas from €3; 🕐noon-4.30pm & 8.30pm-midnight; 🚇La Latina)

Almendro 13

TAPAS €

6 🍴 MAP P54, C2

Almendro 13 is a charming *taberna* (tavern) where you come for traditional Spanish tapas with an emphasis on quality rather than frilly elaborations. Cured meats, cheeses, omelettes and variations on these themes dominate the menu.

It serves both *raciones* (full-plate) and half-sized plates – a full *ración* of the famously good *huevos rotos* ('broken eggs') served with *jamón* (ham) and thin potato slices is a meal in itself. The only problem is that the wait for a table requires the patience of a saint, so order a wine or *manzanilla* (dry sherry) and soak up the buzz. (📞91 365 42 52; www.almendro13.com; Calle del Almendro 13; mains €7-15; 🕐1-4pm & 7.30pm-midnight Sun-Thu, 1-5pm & 8pm-1am Fri & Sat; 🚇La Latina)

Taberna Txakolina

TAPAS €

7 🍴 MAP P54, D2

Taberna Txakolina calls its *pintxos* 'high cuisine in miniature'. If ordering tapas makes you nervous, it couldn't be easier here – they're lined up on the bar, Basque style, in all their glory, and you can simply point. Whatever you order, wash it down with a *txakoli*, a sharp Basque white. (📞91 366 48 77; www.tabernatxacoli.com; Calle de la Cava Baja 26; tapas from €4; 🕐8pm-midnight Tue, 1-4pm & 8pm-midnight Wed-Sat, 1-4pm Sun; 🚇La Latina)

Stew Degustation at Malacatín 🍴

If you can't stomach an entire meal of *cocido a la madrileña* (meat-and-chickpea stew), or if you just want to see what all the fuss is about, head to **Malacatín** (Map p54; D4; 📞91 365 52 41; www.malacatin. com; Calle de Ruda 5; mains €11-15; ⏰11am-5.30pm Mon-Wed & Sat, 11am-5.30pm & 8.15-11pm Thu & Fri, closed Aug; Ⓜ La Latina) where the *degustación de cocido* (taste of *cocido; €5*) at the bar is a great way to try Madrid's favourite dish without going all the way – although locals might say it's a bit like smoking without inhaling.

Taberna Matritum
MODERN SPANISH €€

8 ⊗ MAP P54, D2

This little gem is reason enough to detour from the more popular Calle de la Cava Baja next door. The seasonal menu encompasses terrific tapas, salads and generally creative cooking – try the Catalan sausage and prawn pie or the winter *calçots* (large spring onions), also from Catalonia. The wine list runs into the hundreds and it's sophisticated without being pretentious. (📞91 365 82 37; www. tabernamatritum.es; Calle de la Cava Alta 17; mains €13-19.50; ⏰1.30-4pm & 8.30pm-midnight Wed-Sun, 8.30pm-midnight Mon & Tue; Ⓜ La Latina)

Juana La Loca
TAPAS €€

9 ⊗ MAP P54, C3

Juana La Loca does a range of creative tapas with tempting options lined up along the bar, and more on the menu that they prepare to order. But we love it above all for its brilliant *tortilla de patatas*, which is distinguished from others of its kind by the caramelised onions – simply wonderful. (📞91 366 55 00; www.juanalalocamadrid. com; Plaza de la Puerta de Moros 4; tapas from €4, mains €10-24; ⏰1.30-5.30pm Tue-Sun, 7pm-midnight Sat-Wed, to 1am Thu-Fri; Ⓜ La Latina)

El Estragón
VEGETARIAN €€

10 ⊗ MAP P54, B2

A delightful spot for crêpes, veggie burgers and other vegetarian specialities, El Estragón is undoubtedly one of Madrid's best vegetarian restaurants, although attentive vegans won't appreciate the use of butter. Apart from that, we're yet to hear a bad word about it. (📞91 365 89 82; www.elestragonvegetariano. com; Plaza de la Paja 10; mains €8-15; ⏰1pm-1am; 🥄; Ⓜ La Latina)

Casa Lucio
SPANISH €€€

11 ⊗ MAP P54, D2

Casa Lucio is a Madrid classic and has been wowing *madrileños* with his light touch, quality ingredients and home-style local cooking since 1974, such as eggs (a Lucio speciality) and roasted meats in abundance. There's also *rabo de toro* (bull's tail) during the Fiestas de San Isidro Labrador and plenty of *rioja* (red wine) to wash away the mere thought of it. (📞91 365 32 52, 91 365 82 17; www.casalucio.es; Calle de la Cava Baja 35; mains €18-29; 🕑1-4pm & 8.30pm-midnight, closed Aug; Ⓜ La Latina)

Tapas:
A Primer

🍴

Many would argue that tapas are Spain's greatest culinary gift to the world. While devotees of paella and *jamón* (ham) can make a convincing counterclaim, what clinches it for us is the fact that the potential variety of tapas is endless.

Anything can be a *tapa* (a single item of tapas), from a handful of olives or a slice of *jamón* on bread to a *tortilla de patatas* (Spanish potato omelette) served in liquefied form. That's because tapas is the canvas upon which Spanish chefs paint the story of a nation's obsession with food, the means by which they show their fidelity to traditional Spanish tastes even as they gently nudge their compatriots in previously unimagined directions. By making the most of very little, tapas serves as a link to the impoverished Madrid of centuries past. By re-imagining even the most sacred Spanish staples, tapas is the culinary trademark of a confident country rushing headlong into the future.

Tapas Etiquette

To many visitors, ordering tapas can seem like one of the dark arts of Spanish etiquette. Fear not: in many bars in Madrid, it couldn't be easier. With so many tapas varieties lined up along the bar, you either take a small plate and help yourself or point to the morsel you want. In such cases, it's customary to keep track of what you eat (by holding on to the toothpicks for example) and then tell the bar staff how many you've had when it's time to pay.

Otherwise, many places have a list of tapas, either on a menu or posted up behind the bar. If you can't choose, ask for *la especialidad de la casa* (the house speciality) and it's hard to go wrong. Another way of eating tapas is to order *raciones* (literally 'rations'; large tapas servings) or *media raciones* (half-rations; smaller tapas servings). These plates and half-plates of a particular dish are a good way to go if you particularly like something and want more than a mere *tapa*. Remember, however, that after one or two *raciones* most people are almost certainly full.

Sardines at El Rastro 🍴

There are few more enduring local traditions than *sardinas a la plancha* (sardines cooked on the grill) at **Bar Santurce** (Map p54, E4; 📞646 238303; www. barsanturce.com; Plaza General Vara del Rey 14; bocadillos/raciones from €2.50/4.50; 🕐noon-4pm Tue & Wed, noon-4pm & 7.30-10.30pm Thu-Sat, 9am-4pm Sun; Ⓜ La Latina); during El Rastro it can be difficult to even get near the bar. Then step next door to the tiny and equally beloved Aceitunas Jiménez, purveyor of pickled olives, eggplants, garlic and anything else they've decided to pickle, served in plastic cups.

Posada de la Villa   SPANISH €€€

12 🍴 MAP P54, D2

This wonderfully restored 17th-century *posada* (inn) is something of a local landmark. The atmosphere is formal, the decoration sombre and traditional (heavy timber and brickwork), and the cuisine decidedly local – roast meats, *cocido* (which usually needs to be pre-ordered), *callos* (tripe) and *sopa de ajo* (garlic soup). (📞91 366 18 80; www.posadadelavilla.com; Calle de la Cava Baja 9; mains €21-32.50; 🕐1-4pm & 8pm-midnight Mon-Sat, 1-4pm Sun, closed Aug; Ⓜ La Latina)

Drinking

Taberna El Tempranillo   WINE BAR

13 🍴 MAP P54, C3

You could come here for the tapas, but we recommend Taberna El Tempranillo primarily for its wines, of which it has a selection that puts numerous Spanish bars to shame. It's not a late-night place, but it's always packed in the early evening and on Sunday after El Rastro. Many wines are sold by the glass. (📞91 364 15 32; Calle de la Cava Baja 38; 🕐1-4pm Mon, 1-4pm & 8pm-midnight Tue-Sun; Ⓜ La Latina)

Delic   BAR

14 🍴 MAP P54, B2

We could go on for hours about this long-standing cafe-bar, but we'll reduce it to its most basic elements: nursing an exceptionally good mojito or three on a warm summer's evening at Delic's outdoor tables on one of Madrid's prettiest plazas is one of life's great pleasures. Bliss. (📞91 364 54 50; www.delic.es; Costanilla de San Andrés 14; 🕐11am-2am Sun & Tue-Thu, to 2.30am Fri & Sat; Ⓜ La Latina)

El Eucalipto   COCKTAIL BAR

15 🍴 MAP P54, H5

This fine little bar is devoted to all things Cuban – from the music to the clientele and the Caribbean cocktails (including nonalcoholic), it's a sexy, laid-back place. Not surprisingly, the mojitos are a cut above average, but the juices and daiquiris also have a loyal following. (91 527 27 63; www. facebook.com/eeucalipto; Calle de Argumosa 4; ⏱5pm-2am Sun-Thu, to 3am Fri & Sat; MLavapiés)

Boconó Specialty Coffee CAFE

16 ☕ MAP P54, E3

Close attention to every detail makes Boconó unique – coffee is roasted on-site and fanatics have a choice of styles: espresso, Aero-Press and Chemex, among others. Coffee is weighed before brewing and water is dosed out by the millilitre. The decor is minimal, with reclaimed wood and rough brick, the wi-fi is fast and the service is friendly. (91 040 20 19; www. bocono.es; Calle de los Embajadores 3; coffee €1.60-3; ⏱8.30am-8.30pm

Mon-Thu, to 9pm Fri & Sat, 9.30am-8.30pm Sun; 🛜; MLa Latina)

Entertainment

Casa Patas FLAMENCO

17 ⭐ MAP P54, H2

One of the top flamenco stages in Madrid, this *tablao* (choreographed flamenco show) always offers flaw-less quality that serves as a good introduction to the art. It's not the friendliest place in town, especially if you're only here for the show, and you're likely to be crammed in a little, but no one complains about the standard of the performances. (91 369 04 96; www.casapatas.com; Calle de Cañizares 10; admission incl drink €38; ⏱shows 10.30pm Mon-Thu, 8pm & 10.30pm Fri & Sat; MAntón Martín, Tirso de Molina)

Delic

Corral de la Morería FLAMENCO

18 ⭐ MAP P54, A2

This is one of the most prestigious flamenco stages in Madrid, with 50 years of experience as a leading venue and top performers most nights. The stage area has a rustic feel, and tables are pushed up close. Set menus from €45 (additional to the admission fee). (🕿 91 365 84 46; www.corraldelamoreria. com; Calle de la Morería 17; admission incl drink from €45; ⏰7pm-12.15am, shows 8.30pm & 10.20pm; Ⓜ Ópera)

Café Ziryab FLAMENCO

19 ⭐ MAP P54, E6

For a fine, well-priced flamenco show that draws as many locals as tourists, Café Ziryab is a bit out of the city centre but worth the excursion. At 11pm on Fridays, the *peña flamenca* is a jam session for those who feel the urge and, when it works, is authentic flamenco at its improvised, soul-stirring best. (🕿91 219 29 02; www.cafeziryab.com; Paseo de la Esperanza 17; adult/child €22/8; ⏰shows 9.30pm Wed-Mon; Ⓜ Acacias)

ContraClub LIVE MUSIC

20 ⭐ MAP P54, A2

ContraClub is a crossover live music venue and nightclub, with an eclectic mix of live music (pop, rock, indie, singer-songwriter, blues etc). After the live acts (from 10pm), resident DJs serve up equally diverse beats (indie, pop, funk and soul) to make sure you

don't move elsewhere. (🕿91 365 55 45; www.contraclub.es; Calle de Bailén 16; entrance €3-15; ⏰10pm-6am Wed-Sat; Ⓜ La Latina)

Shopping

Botería Julio Rodríguez ARTS & CRAFTS

21 🔒 MAP P54, B4

One of the last makers of traditional Spanish wineskins left in Madrid, Botería Julio Rodríguez is like a window on a fast-disappearing world. They make a great gift and, as you'd expect, they're in a different league from the cheap wineskins found in souvenir shops across downtown Madrid. (🕿91 365 66 29; www.boteriajuliorodriguez. es; Calle del Águila 12; ⏰9.30am-2pm & 4.30-8pm Mon-Fri, 10am-1.30pm Sat; Ⓜ La Latina)

Helena Rohner JEWELLERY

22 🔒 MAP P54, D2

One of Europe's most creative jewellery designers, Helena Rohner has a spacious boutique in La Latina. Working with silver, stone, porcelain, wood and Murano glass, she makes inventive pieces that are a regular feature of Paris fashion shows. In her own words, she seeks to recreate 'the magic of Florence, the vitality of London and the luminosity of Madrid'. (🕿91 365 79 06; www.helenarohner.com; Calle del Almendro 4; ⏰9am-8.30pm Mon-Fri, noon-2.30pm & 3.30-8pm Sat, noon-3pm Sun; Ⓜ La Latina, Tirso de Molina)

MARK READ/LONELY PLANET ©

Flamenco dancers performing at Corral de la Morería

Aceitunas Jiménez

FOOD

23  MAP P54, D4

An institution on a Sunday stroll in El Rastro, this tiny shop serves up pickled olives in plastic cups and in all manner of varieties, as well as aubergines, garlic and anything else they've decided to soak in lashings of oil and/or vinegar. (☎91 365 46 23; Plaza del General Vara del Rey 14; ⏰10.30am-2.30pm & 3.30-8pm Mon-Thu, 10.30am-2.30pm Fri & Sat, 10.30am-3pm Sun; Ⓜ La Latina)

De Piedra

JEWELLERY

24  MAP P54, D3

Necklaces, earrings, bracelets and home decorations made by a local design team fill this lovely showroom. Silver and semiprecious stones are the mainstays. (☎91 365 96 20; www.depiedracreaciones. com; Calle de la Ruda 19; ⏰11am-2pm & 5-8.30pm Mon-Sat, noon-3pm Sun; Ⓜ La Latina)

Walking Tour 🚶

Architectural Madrid

Madrid may not have the Eiffel Tower, Colosseum or Sagrada Família, but it is easily the rival of Paris, Rome or Barcelona for its astonishing grand monuments. From the heart of old Madrid where the city was born to the showpiece architecture of 19th- and 20th-century Spain, this walk takes you through the Spanish capital's splendid architectural attractions.

Walk Facts

Start Plaza de la Villa;
Ⓜ Ópera

End Antigua Estación de Atocha; Ⓜ Atocha Renfe

Length 5km; two to three hours

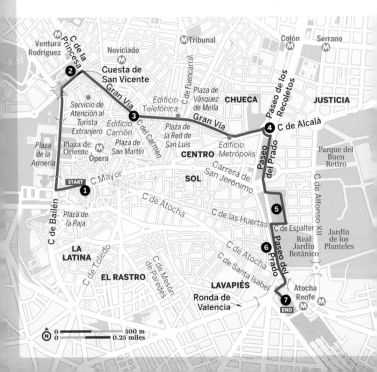

❶ Plaza de la Villa

This compact square (p42) hosts a lovely collection of 17th-century Madrid architecture. The brickwork and slate spires are the most distinctive characteristics of a style known as Madrid baroque (*barroco madrileño*).

❷ Plaza de España

Towering over this square on the east side is the Edificio de España, which clearly sprang from the totalitarian recesses of Franco's imagination such is its resemblance to austere Soviet monumentalism. To the north stands the 35-storey Torre de Madrid, another important landmark on the Madrid skyline.

❸ Gran Vía

The iconic Gran Vía is defined by towering belle époque facades. Eye-catching buildings include the Carrión, Madrid's first tower-block apartment hotel; the 1920s-era Telefónica building used for target practice during the Civil War; and the French-designed 1905 Edificio Metrópolis (p72).

❹ Plaza de la Cibeles

Madrid's most striking roundabout is a stirring celebration of the belle époque from the early 20th century. In addition to the extraordinary Palacio de Comunicaciones (1917), the Palacio de Linares, Palacio Buenavista and Banco de España (1891) all watch over the square.

❺ Museo del Prado

The building in which the Prado (p86) is housed is itself an architectural masterpiece. The western wing was designed by Juan de Villanueva, a towering figure of 18th-century Spanish culture and an architect who left his mark across the capital (eg the Plaza Mayor).

❻ Caixa Forum

Caixa Forum (p103), along the Paseo del Prado, is Madrid's most unusual example of contemporary architecture. Its vertical garden, seeming absence of supporting pillars and wrought-iron roof are unlike anything you'll see elsewhere.

❼ Antigua Estación de Atocha

The northwestern wing of Atocha train station was artfully overhauled in 1992. This grand iron-and-glass relic from the 19th century was preserved while its interior was converted into a light-filled tropical garden. It's a thoroughly modern space that nonetheless resonates with the stately European train stations of another age.

✖ Take a Break

Across the other side of the Paseo del Prado, Estado Puro (p104) is one of Madrid's most exciting tapas bars, with innovative twists on traditional Spanish mainstays.

Explore ⊛
Sol, Santa Ana & Huertas

These tightly packed streets are best known for night-life that doesn't seem to abate once the sun goes down, but there's also the beguiling Plaza de Santa Ana, a stirring literary heritage in the Barrio de las Letras and, at the Sol end of things, Madrid's beating heart, you'll find the sum total of all Madrid's personalities, with fabulous shopping, eating and entertainment options.

Sol, Santa Ana and Huertas together make up Madrid's most clamorous corner. Many explorations of this neighbourhood begin in the Plaza de la Puerta del Sol, the pulsing heart of downtown Madrid, then move on to nearby Plaza de Santa Ana and the laneways that tumble down the hillside to the east.

Sol is above all a crossroads, a place for people to meet before fanning out across the city. There are reasons to linger, but for the most part a sense of transience is what prevails. Plaza de Santa Ana, on the other hand, is a destination in its own right, a beautiful square that has become emblematic of a city intent on living the good life. It is also a place of many moods. On a sunny weekday afternoon, it can be quiet, but come most nights of the week, Santa Ana and the surrounding streets crescendo into life.

Getting There

Ⓜ The Sol metro station is one of the city's most useful, with lines 1, 2 and 3 all passing through. Other useful stations are Sevilla (line 2) and Tirso de Molina and Antón Martín (both line 1).

Neighbourhood Map on p70

Plaza de la Puerta del Sol (p72) LUCVI/SHUTTERSTOCK ©

Walking Tour 🚶

A Night Out in Huertas

As sunset nears, locals begin arriving in the Plaza de Santa Ana and the streets towards Sol and down towards the Paseo del Prado. That's because bars here range from cool and classy rooftop perches to ancient barrio (district) classics that haven't changed in decades. And thrown in for good measure is arguably Madrid's finest collection of live-music venues.

Walk Facts

Start Plaza de Santa Ana;
Ⓜ Antón Martín, Sol

End La Terraza del Urban;
Ⓜ Sevilla

Length 3.5km; three to five hours

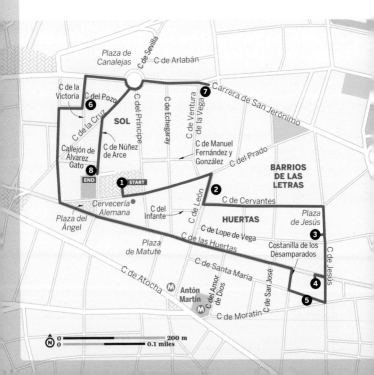

❶ Plaza de Santa Ana

So many Huertas nights begin on this iconic Madrid square, surrounded as it is by so many bars with outdoor tables. Start wherever there's a free table on the square, but Cervecería Alemana (p78) has a Hemingway history.

❷ Casa Pueblo

A storied Huertas bar that prides itself on free live jazz and a bohemian outlook, **Casa Pueblo** (☏91 420 20 38; www.facebook.com/casapueblobar; Calle de León 3; ☉5pm-2am Mon-Thu, 3pm-3am Fri, 3pm-3am Sat, 3pm-2am Sun; Ⓜ Antón Martín, Banco de España) serves up a winning combination of cakes and cocktails, and draws an in-the-know 30-something crowd.

❸ Taberna La Dolores

Old bottles and beer mugs line the shelves at this Madrid institution. The 30-something crowd often includes the odd *famoso* (celebrity) or two. **Taberna La Dolores** (☏91 429 22 43; Plaza de Jesús 4; ☉11am-1am; Ⓜ Antón Martín) claims to be 'the most famous bar in Madrid' – it's invariably full, so who are we to argue?

❹ Maceiras

Key to surviving long Madrid nights is never to drink on an empty stomach, and the Galician tapas (think octopus, green peppers) in Maceiras (p74), a rustic bar down the Huertas hill, are outstanding. Wash it down with a crisp white Ribeiro and you're halfway to being a local.

❺ Jazz Bar

Jazz aficionados begin the night at **Jazz Bar** (☏91 429 70 31; Calle de Moratín 35; ☉3pm-2.30am; Ⓜ Antón Martín) before heading on to live performances elsewhere. With an endless jazz soundtrack, discreet leather booths and plenty of greenery, it's not surprising many return later in the night.

❻ Taberna Alhambra

There can be a certain sameness about the bars between Sol and Huertas, which is why this fine old **taberna** (☏91 521 07 08; Calle de la Victoria 9; ☉11am-1am Sun-Wed, to 2am Thu, to 2.30am Fri & Sat; Ⓜ Sol) stands out. The striking facade and exquisite tile work of the interior are quite beautiful; however, this place is anything but stuffy and the feel is cool, casual and busy.

❼ La Terraza del Urban

A strong contender for best rooftop bar in Madrid, this indulgent terrace (p77) sits atop the five-star Urban Hotel and has five-star views with five-star prices – worth every euro. It's only open while the weather's warm.

❽ Villa Rosa

Villa Rosa (p80), with its extravagantly tiled facade, has been going strong since 1914, and in that time it has seen many manifestations. It originally made its name as a flamenco venue and has recently returned to its roots with well-priced shows and meals that won't break the bank.

N 0 ____ 200 m
0 ____ 0.1 miles

For reviews see

◉	Sights	p71
✕	Eating	p72
🍷	Drinking	p76
✿	Entertainment	p78
🔒	Shopping	p80

Sights

Real Academia de Bellas Artes de San Fernando MUSEUM

1 ◉ MAP P70, B3

The Real Academia de Bellas Artes, Madrid's 'other' art gallery, has for centuries played a pivotal role in the artistic life of the city. As the royal fine arts academy, it has nurtured local talent, thereby complementing the royal penchant for drawing the great international artists of the day into their realm. The pantheon of former alumni reads like a who's who of Spanish art, and the collection that now hangs on the academy's walls is a suitably rich one. (☎91 524 08 64; www.realacademiabellasartessan fernando.com; Calle de Alcalá 13; adult/child €8/free, Wed free; ⏰10am-3pm Tue-Sun Sep-Jul; Ⓜ Sol, Sevilla)

Círculo de Bellas Artes ARTS CENTRE, VIEWPOINT

2 ◉ MAP P70, D2

For some of Madrid's best views, take the lift to the 7th floor of the 'Fine Arts Circle'. You can almost reach out and touch the glorious dome of the Edificio Metrópolis and otherwise take in Madrid in all its finery, including the distant mountains. Two bars, lounge music and places to recline add to the experience. Downstairs, the centre has exhibitions, concerts, short films and book readings.

There's also a fine belle-époque cafe (p77) on the ground floor. (La Azotea; ☎91 360 54 00; www.circulobellasartes.com; Calle de Alcalá 42; admission to roof terrace €4; ⏰roof terrace 9am-2am Mon-Thu, to 3am Fri, 11am-3am Sat, 11am-2am Sun; Ⓜ Banco de España, Sevilla)

Plaza de Santa Ana SQUARE

3 ◉ MAP P70, B4

Plaza de Santa Ana is a delightful confluence of elegant architecture and irresistible energy. It presides over the upper reaches of the Barrio de las Letras (p72) and this literary personality makes its presence felt with the statues of the 17th-century writer Calderón de la Barca and Federíco García Lorca, and in the **Teatro Español** (☎91 360 14 84; www.teatroespanol. es; Calle del Príncipe 25; Ⓜ Sevilla, Sol, Antón Martín) at the plaza's eastern end. Apart from anything else, the plaza is the starting point for many a long Huertas night.

The plaza was laid out in 1810 during the controversial reign of Joseph Bonaparte (elder brother of Napoleon), giving breathing space to what had hitherto been one of Madrid's most claustrophobic *barrios*. The plaza quickly became a focal point for intellectual life, and the cafes surrounding the plaza thronged with writers, poets and artists engaging in endless *tertulias* (literary and philosophical discussions). (Ⓜ Sevilla, Sol, Antón Martín)

It's Free

The Real Academia de Bellas Artes de San Fernando (p71) has a collection the envy of many a European gallery, and it's free to enjoy if you come on a Wednesday.

Edificio Metrópolis

ARCHITECTURE

4 ⊙ MAP P70, D2

Among the more interesting buildings along Gran Vía is the stunning, French-designed Edificio Metrópolis, built in 1905, which marks the southern end of Gran Vía. The winged victory statue atop its dome was added in 1975 and is best seen from Calle de Alcalá or Plaza de la Cibeles. It's magnificent when floodlit. (Gran Vía; **M** Banco de España, Sevilla)

Plaza de la Puerta del Sol

SQUARE

5 ⊙ MAP P70, A3

The official centre point of Spain is a gracious, crowded hemisphere of elegant facades. It is, above all, a crossroads: people here are forever heading somewhere else, on foot, by metro (three lines cross here) or by bus (many lines terminate and start nearby). Hard as it is to believe now, in Madrid's earliest days, the Puerta del Sol (Gate of the Sun) was the eastern gate of the city. (**M** Sol)

Barrio de las Letras

AREA

6 ⊙ MAP P70, D4

The area that unfurls down the hill east of Plaza de Santa Ana is referred to as the Barrio de las Letras because of the writers who lived here during Spain's golden age of the 16th and 17th centuries. Miguel de Cervantes Saavedra (1547–1616), the author of *Don Quijote,* spent much of his adult life in Madrid and lived and died at **Calle de Cervantes 2**; a plaque (dating from 1834) sits above the door. (District of Letters; **M** Antón Martín)

Hammam al-Andalus

SPA

7 ⊙ MAP P70, A5

Housed in the excavated cellars of old Madrid, this imitation of a traditional Arab bath offers massages and aromatherapy beneath graceful arches, accompanied by the sound of trickling water. Prices are cheapest from 10am to 4pm Monday to Friday; reservations required. (📞 91 429 90 20; http://madrid.hammamalandalus.com; Calle de Atocha 14; treatments €33-115; 🕙 10am-midnight; **M** Sol)

Eating

Casa Labra

TAPAS €

8 ⊗ MAP P70, A3

Casa Labra has been going strong since 1860, an era that the decor strongly evokes. Locals love their *bacalao* (cod) and ordering it here – either as deep-fried tapas (*una tajada de bacalao* goes for

€1.50) or *una croqueta de bacalao* (€1.50) – is a Madrid rite of initiation. As the lunchtime queues attest, they go through more than 700kg of cod every week. (📞91 532 14 05; www.casalabra.es; Calle de Tetuán 11; tapas from €1; 🕒11.30am-3.30pm & 6-11pm; Ⓜ Sol)

Casa Toni SPANISH €

9 ❌ MAP P70, B4

Locals flock to Casa Toni, one of Madrid's best old-school Spanish bars, for simple, honest cuisine fresh off the griddle. Specialities include cuttlefish, gazpacho and offal – the crispy pork ear is out of this world. While you're there, you can try one of the local Madrid wines. The prices are great and the old Madrid charm can't be beat. (📞91 532 25 80; casatoni2@hotmail.com; Calle de la Cruz 14; mains €6-13; 🕒noon-4.30pm & 7pm-midnight; Ⓜ Sol)

Vinos González TAPAS, DELI €

10 ❌ MAP P70, C5

Ever dreamed of a deli where you could choose a tasty morsel and sit down and eat it right there? Well, the two are usually kept separate in Spain but here you can. On offer is a tempting array of local and international cheeses, cured meats and other typically Spanish delicacies. The tables are informal, cafe style and we recommend lingering. (📞91 429 56 18; www.casagonzalez.es; Calle de León 12; tapas from €3.50, raciones €9-15; 🕒9.30am-midnight Mon-Thu, to 1am Fri & Sat, 11am-6pm Sun; Ⓜ Antón Martín)

Plaza de Santa Ana (p71)

CHRISTIAN MUELLER/SHUTTERSTOCK ©

Sol, Santa Ana & Huertas Eating

El Lateral

TAPAS €

11 ❌ MAP P70, B5

Our pick of the bars surrounding Plaza de Santa Ana, El Lateral does terrific *pinchos* (snacks), the perfect accompaniment to the fine wines on offer. Tapas are creative without being over the top (wild mushroom croquettes or sirloin with foie gras). Service is restaurant-standard, rather than your average tapas-bar brusqueness. (📞91 420 15 82; www.lateral.com; Plaza de Santa Ana 12; tapas €1.55-9.80, raciones €7-13; 🕐noon-midnight Sun-Wed, to 2am Thu-Sat; Ⓜ Antón Martín, Sol)

Casa Alberto

TAPAS €€

12 ❌ MAP P70, C5

One of the most atmospheric old *tabernas* (taverns) of Madrid, Casa Alberto has been around since 1827 and occupies a building where Cervantes is said to have written one of his books. The secret to its staying power is vermouth on tap, excellent tapas at the bar and fine sit-down meals. (📞91 429 93 56; www.casaalberto. es; Calle de las Huertas 18; tapas €3.25-10, raciones €7-16.50, mains €16-19; 🕐restaurant 1.30-4pm & 8pm-midnight Tue-Sat, 1.30-4pm Sun, bar noon-1.30am Tue-Sat, 12.30-4pm Sun, closed Sun Jul & Aug; Ⓜ Antón Martín)

Maceiras

GALICIAN €€

13 ❌ MAP P70, D5

Galician tapas (octopus, green peppers etc) never tasted so good

Pastry Stop 🍽️

Right on Sol, **La Mallorquina** (Map p70, A3; 📞91 521 12 01; www.pasteleriamallorquina. es; Plaza de la Puerta del Sol 8; pastries from €2; 🕐9am-9.15pm; Ⓜ Sol) is a classic pastry shop that's packed to the rafters by locals who just couldn't pass by without stopping. The most popular order is an *ensaimada* (a light pastry dusted with icing sugar) from Mallorca.

as in this agreeably rustic bar down the bottom of the Huertas hill, especially when washed down with a crisp white Ribeiro. The simple wooden tables, loyal customers, Galician music playing in the background and handy location make it a fine place for before or after visiting the museums along the Paseo del Prado.

There's another **branch** (Calle de Jesús 7) around the corner. (📞91 429 58 18; www.tabernamaceira.com; Calle de las Huertas 66; mains €6-14; 🕐1.15-4.15pm & 8pm-midnight Mon-Thu, 1.30-4.45pm & 8.30pm-1am Fri & Sat, 1.30-4.45pm & 8pm-midnight Sun; Ⓜ Antón Martín)

La Mucca de Prado

SPANISH, INTERNATIONAL €€

14 ❌ MAP P70, C4

This wildly popular outpost of the similarly cool Malasaña La Mucca serves up terrific local dishes such as *jamón* (ham) platters, but the menu is mostly international with pizzas, steaks, burgers and salads, usually with a Spanish twist. The food is great, but there's also an irresistible buzz about this place that makes everything taste better and the night last longer. (☎91 521 00 00; www.lamuccacompany.com/lamucca-de-prado; Calle del Prado 16; mains €9-16; ☉1pm-1.30am Sun-Wed, to 2am Thu, to 2.30am Fri & Sat; Ⓜ Antón Martín)

Los Gatos   TAPAS €€

🅖 ⊗ MAP P70, D5

Tapas you can point to without deciphering the menu and eclectic old-world decor (from bullfighting memorabilia to a fresco of skeletons at the bar) make this a popular choice down the bottom end of Huertas. The most popular orders are the *canapés* (tapas on toast), which, we have to say, are rather delicious. (☎91 429 30 67; Calle de Jesús 2; tapas from €3.75; ☉11am-2am; Ⓜ Antón Martín)

La Terraza del Casino   MODERN SPANISH €€€

🅗 ⊗ MAP P70, C3

Perched atop the lavish Casino de Madrid building, this temple of haute cuisine is the proud bearer of two Michelin stars and presided over by celebrity chef Paco Roncero. It's all about culinary experimentation, with a menu that changes as each new idea emerges from the laboratory and moves into the kitchen. The *menú de degustación* (€148) is a fabulous avalanche of tastes. (☎91 532 12 75; www.casinodemadrid.es; Calle

Lhardy (p76)

de Alcalá 15; mains €44-56, set menus €79-185; ⏱1-4pm & 9pm-midnight Mon-Sat; Ⓜ Sevilla)

Lhardy

SPANISH €€€

17 ❌ MAP P70, B3

This Madrid landmark (since 1839) is an elegant treasure trove of takeaway gourmet tapas downstairs and six dining areas upstairs that are the upmarket preserve of traditional Madrid dishes with an occasional hint of French influence. House specialities include *cocido a la madrileña* (meat-and-chickpea stew), pheasant and wild duck in an orange perfume. The quality and service are unimpeachable. (☎91 521 33 85; www.lhardy.com; Carrera de San Jerónimo 8; mains €24-36; ⏱1-3.30pm & 8.30-11pm Mon-Sat, 1-3.30pm Sun, closed Aug; Ⓜ Sol, Sevilla)

Drinking

La Venencia

BAR

18 🍺 MAP P70, C4

La Venencia is a *barrio* classic, with *manzanilla* (chamomile-coloured sherry) from Sanlúcar and sherry from Jeréz poured straight from the dusty wooden barrels, accompanied by a small selection of tapas with an Andalucian bent. There's no music, no flashy decorations; here it's all about you, your *fino* (sherry) and your friends. (☎91 429 73 13; Calle de Echegaray 7; ⏱12.30-3.30pm & 7.30pm-1.30am; Ⓜ Sol, Sevilla)

Salmón Gurú

COCKTAIL BAR

19 🍺 MAP P70, C4

When Sergi Arola's empire collapsed and the celebrated Le Cabrera cocktail bar went with it, Madrid lost one of its best cocktail maestros, Diego Cabrera. Thankfully, he's back with a wonderful multifaceted space where he serves up a masterful collection of drinks – work your way through his menu of 25 Cabrera *clasicos* to get started. (☎91 000 61 85; http://salmonguru.es; Calle de Echegaray 21; ⏱5pm-2.30am Wed-Sun; Ⓜ Antón Martín)

Tartân Roof

LOUNGE

20 🍺 MAP P70, D3

Order a cocktail, then lie down on the cushions and admire the vista from this fabulous rooftop terrace. It's a brilliant place to chill out, with the views at their best close to sunset. (La Azotea; www.azoteadel circulo.com; 7th fl, Calle Marqués de Casa Riera 2; admission €4; ⏱9am-2am Mon-Thu, to 2.30am Fri, 11am-2.30am Sat & Sun)

El Imperfecto

COCKTAIL BAR

21 🍺 MAP P70, C5

Its name notwithstanding, the 'Imperfect One' is our ideal Huertas bar, with occasional live jazz and a drinks menu as long as a saxophone, ranging from cocktails (€7, or two mojitos for €10) and spirits to milkshakes, teas and creative coffees. Its pina colada is one of the best we've tasted and the atmosphere is agreeably buzzy yet chilled. (Plaza de Matute 2; ⏱5pm-2.30am Mon-Thu, 3pm-2.30am Fri & Sat; Ⓜ Antón Martín)

La Terraza del Urban COCKTAIL BAR

22 🚇 MAP P70, C4

A strong contender for best roof-top bar in Madrid, this indulgent terrace sits atop the five-star Urban Hotel and has five-star views with five-star prices – worth every euro. It's only open while the weather's warm. (📞 91 787 77 70; Carrera de San Jerónimo 34, Urban Hotel; ⏱noon-8pm Sun & Mon, to 3am Tue-Sat mid-May–Sep; Ⓜ Sevilla)

Café del Círculo de Bellas Artes CAFE

23 🚇 MAP P70, D2

This wonderful belle-époque cafe was designed by Antonio Palacios in 1919 and boasts chandeliers and the charm of a bygone era, even if the waiters are not averse to looking aggrieved if you put them out. That said, they're friendlier than they used to be! (📞 91 521 69 42; Calle de Alcalá 42; ⏱9am-1am Sun-Thu, to 3am Fri & Sat; Ⓜ Banco de España, Sevilla)

Viva Madrid BAR

24 🚇 MAP P70, C4

The tiled facade of Viva Madrid is one of Madrid's most recognisable and it's an essential landmark on the Huertas nightlife scene.

La Terraza del Casino (p75)

INGOLF POMPE 85/ALAMY STOCK PHOTO ©

Packed to the rafters on weekends, come here for fine mojitos and the casual, friendly atmosphere. The tapas offerings are another reason to pass by. (📞91 420 35 96; www.restaurantevivamadrid.com; Calle de Manuel Fernández y González 7; ⏱noon-midnight Mon-Thu, to 2am Fri & Sat; Ⓜ Antón Martín, Sol)

Cervecería Alemana   BAR

25 📍 MAP P70, B5

If you've only got time to stop at one bar on Plaza de Santa Ana, let it be this classic *cervecería* (beer bar), renowned for its cold, frothy beers and a wider selection of Spanish beers than is the norm. It's fine inside, but snaffle a table outside in the plaza on a summer's evening and you won't be giving it up without a fight.

Opened in 1904, this was one of Hemingway's haunts – neither the wood-lined bar nor the bow-tied waiters have changed much since his day. (📞91 429 70 33; www.cerveceriaalemana.com; Plaza de Santa Ana 6; ⏱11am-12.30am Sun-Thu, to 2am Fri & Sat, closed Aug; Ⓜ Antón Martín, Sol)

Entertainment

Sala El Sol   LIVE MUSIC

26 📍 MAP P70, B2

Madrid institutions don't come any more beloved than the terrific Sala El Sol. It opened in 1979, just in time for *la movida madrileña* (the Madrid scene), and quickly established itself as a leading stage for all the icons of the era, such as Nacha Pop and Alaska y los Pegamoides. (📞91 532 64 90; www.elsolmad.com; Calle de los Jardines 3, admission incl drink €10, concert tickets €6-30; ⏱midnight-5.30am Tue-Sat Jul-Sep; Ⓜ Gran Vía)

Café Central   JAZZ

27 📍 MAP P70, B5

In 2011 the respected jazz magazine *Down Beat* included this art-deco bar on the list of the world's best jazz clubs, the only place in Spain to earn the prestigious accolade (said by some to be the jazz equivalent of earning a Michelin star). With well over 1000 gigs under its belt, it rarely misses a beat. (📞91 369 41 43; www.cafecentralmadrid.com; Plaza del Ángel 10; admission €12-18; ⏱12.30pm-2.30am Mon-Thu, to 3.30am Fri, 11.30am-3.30am Sat, performances 9pm; Ⓜ Antón Martín, Sol)

Teatro de la Zarzuela   THEATRE

28 📍 MAP P70, D3

This theatre, built in 1856, is the premier place to see *zarzuela* (Spanish mix of theatre, music and dance). It also hosts a smattering of classical music and opera, as well as the cutting edge Compañía Nacional de Danza. (📞91 524 54 00; www.teatrodelazarzuela.mcu.es; Calle de Jovellanos 4; tickets €5-60; ⏱box office noon-6pm Mon-Fri, 3-6pm Sat & Sun; Ⓜ Banco de España, Sevilla)

Pedro Almodóvar

La Movida Madrileña

Born in a small, impoverished village in Castilla-La Mancha, Almodóvar once remarked that in such conservative rural surrounds, 'I felt as if I'd fallen from another planet'. After he moved to Madrid in 1969 he found his spiritual home and began his career making underground Super-8 movies and making a living by selling secondhand goods at El Rastro flea market. His early films *Pepi, Luci, Bom y otras chicas del montón* (Pepi, Luci, Bom and the Other Girls; 1980) and *Laberinto de pasiones* (Labyrinth of Passions; 1982) – the film that brought a young Antonio Banderas to attention – announced him as the icon of *la movida madrileña* (the Madrid scene), the explosion of hedonism and creativity in the early years of post-Franco Spain. Almodóvar had both in bucketloads; he peppered his films with candy-bright colours and characters leading lives where sex and drugs were the norm. By night Almodóvar performed in Madrid's most famous *movida* bars as part of a drag act called Almodóvar & McNamara. He even appeared in this latter role in *Laberinto de pasiones*.

Later Work

By the mid-1980s *madrileños* (people from Madrid) had adopted him as one of the city's most famous sons and he went on to broaden his fanbase with quirkily comic looks at modern Spain, generally set in the capital, such as *Mujeres al borde de un ataque de nervios* (Women on the Verge of a Nervous Breakdown; 1988) and *¡Átame!* (Tie Me Up! Tie Me Down!; 1990). *Todo sobre mi madre* (All About My Mother; 1999) won Almodóvar his first Oscar for Best Foreign Film and is also notable for the coming of age of the Madrid-born actress Penélope Cruz, who had starred in a number of Almodóvar films and was considered part of a select group of the director's leading ladies long before she became a Hollywood star. Other outstanding movies in a formidable portfolio include *Tacones lejanos* (High Heels; 1991) in which Villa Rosa (p80) makes an appearance; *Hable con ella* (Talk to Her; 2002), for which he won a Best Original Screenplay Oscar; and *Volver* (Return; 2006), which reunited Almodóvar with Penélope Cruz to popular and critical acclaim.

Villa Rosa
FLAMENCO

29 ⭐ MAP P70, B4

Villa Rosa has been going strong since 1914, and in that time it has seen many manifestations. It originally made its name as a flamenco venue and has recently returned to its roots with well-priced shows and meals.

The extraordinary tiled facade (1928) is the work of Alfonso Romero, who was also responsible for the tile work in the Plaza de Toros – the facade is a tourist attraction in itself. This long-standing nightclub even appeared in the Pedro Almodóvar film *Tacones lejanos* (High Heels; 1991). (📞91 521 36 89; www.reservas.tablao flamencovillarosa.com; Plaza de Santa Ana 15; admission incl drink adult/child €35/17; ⏰11pm-6am Mon-Sat, shows 8.30pm & 10.45pm; Ⓜ Sol)

Costello Café & Niteclub
LIVE MUSIC

30 ⭐ MAP P70, B2

The very cool Costello Café & Niteclub weds smooth-as-silk ambience to an innovative mix of pop, rock and fusion in Warholesque surrounds. There's live music (pop and rock, often of the indie variety) at 9.30pm every night except Sunday and Monday, with resident and visiting DJs keeping you on your feet until closing time the rest of the week. (📞91 522 18 15; www.

costelloclub.com; Calle del Caballero de Gracia 10; €8-20; ⏰8pm-2.30am Tue, to 3am Wed & Thu, to 3.30am Fri & Sat; Ⓜ Gran Vía)

Shopping

Licores Cabello
WINE

31 🔒 MAP P70, C4

All wine shops should be like this. This family-run corner shop really knows its wines and the interior has scarcely changed since 1913, with wooden shelves and even a faded ceiling fresco. There are fine wines in abundance (mostly Spanish, and a few foreign bottles), with some 500 labels on show or tucked away out the back. (📞91 429 60 88; Calle de Echegaray 19; ⏰10am-3pm & 5.30-10pm Mon-Sat; Ⓜ Sevilla, Antón Martín)

Casa de Diego
FASHION & ACCESSORIES

32 🔒 MAP P70, A3

This classic shop has been around since 1858, making, selling and repairing Spanish fans, shawls, umbrellas and canes. Service is old style and occasionally grumpy, but the fans are works of antique art. There's another **branch** (📞91 531 02 23; Calle del los Mesoneros Romanos 4; ⏰9.30am-1.30pm & 4.45-8pm Mon-Sat; Ⓜ Callao, Sol) nearby. (📞91 522 66 43; www.casadediego. com; Plaza de la Puerta del Sol 12; ⏰9.30am-8pm Mon-Sat; Ⓜ Sol)

Villa Rosa

Santarrufina
RELIGIOUS

33 🔒 MAP P70, A4

This gilded outpost of Spanish Catholicism has to be seen to be believed. Churches, priests and monasteries are some of the patrons of this overwhelming three-storey shop full of everything from simple rosaries to imposing statues of saints and even a litter used to carry the Virgin in processions. Head downstairs for a peek at the extravagant chapel. (🕿91 522 23 83; www.santarrufina.com; Calle de la Paz 4; ⊗10am-2pm & 4.30-8pm Mon-Fri, 10am-2pm Sat; Ⓜ Sol)

Almacén de Pontejos
CLOTHING

34 🔒 MAP P70, A4

Describing what this shop sells – fabrics, buttons and all manner of knick-knacks for dressmakers – only tells half the story. It's one of many such stores on the square and in the surrounding streets, an intriguing hidden subculture that dates back decades, a stone's throw from the Puerta del Sol. And it's very much alive – these shops can throng with people. (🕿91 521 55 94; www.almacendepontejos.com; Plaza de Pontejos 2; ⊗9.30am-2pm & 4.30-8.15pm Mon-Fri, 9.30am-2pm Sat; Ⓜ Sol)

Walking Tour 🥾

Foodie's Madrid

Food is perhaps the most enduring centrepiece of madrileño (people from Madrid) life. In Madrid, arguably the country's most underrated food city, everything great about Spain's culinary traditions and innovations is present, and it's the diverse culinary experiences on offer that make the city such a wonderful introduction to Spanish cuisine.

Walk Facts

Start Mercado de San Miguel; Ⓜ Sol

End Lhardy; Ⓜ Sol, Sevilla

Length 2km; two to four hours

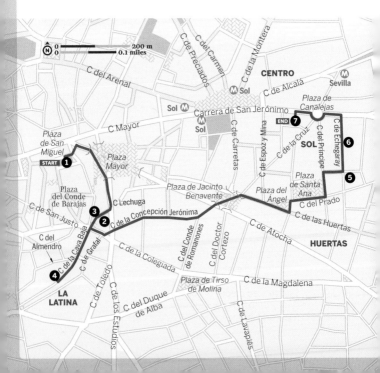

❶ Mercado de San Miguel

This wonderfully converted early 20th-century market (p44) is a gastronome's paradise, with tapas to be enjoyed on the spot (everything from chocolate to caviar), fresh produce at every turn and a buzz that rarely abates until closing time at 2am. La Casa de Bacalao (Stall 17), for example, is a particular favourite.

❷ Casa Revuelta

The decor at Casa Revuelta (p44) hasn't changed in decades, nor has the clientele. They come here for the boneless tapas of *bacalao* (cod) and the convivial air of a Madrid bar where the staff shout to make themselves heard. To understand this city, come here at 1pm Sunday.

❸ Restaurante Sobrino de Botín

This is the world's oldest continuously functioning restaurant (p44). Roasted meats served in a wonderful setting (ask for a table in the vaulted cellar) could easily explain its longevity, but El Botín also appears in novels by Ernest Hemingway, Frederick Forsyth and a host of local writers.

❹ Calle de la Cava Baja

Calle de la Cava Baja's medieval streetscape follows the path of Madrid's long-disappeared medieval wall. It's also one of the great food streets of the world, home to a slew of tapas bars that makes La Latina one of the best places to eat in the country.

❺ Licores Cabello

There are wine shops where a catalogue is handed to you, and then there's Licores Cabello (p80). Staff know their wines here, and they are as comfortable speaking to experts as they are to first-timers keen to sample Spanish wines without knowing where to start.

❻ La Venencia

La Venencia (p76) is the evocation of an old-style Spanish dream. Here staff pour the sherry straight from the barrel, they're not averse to looking grumpy in the honoured tradition of Spanish bartenders and you can almost smell the dust of decades past.

❼ Lhardy

It would be a shame to wander around Madrid with food on your mind and not head in to Lhardy (p76). The ground-floor deli is all about planning a picnic in the Parque del Buen Retiro tomorrow or buying cured meats, cheeses and other delicacies to take back home. Doing so is *very* Madrid.

✕ Take a Break
Chocolatería de San Ginés
(☎ 91 365 65 46; www.chocolateriasangines.com; Pasadizo de San Ginés 5; ⏱ 24hr; Ⓜ Sol)

Explore ✦

El Retiro & the Art Museums

From Plaza de la Cibeles in the north, the buildings arrayed along Paseo del Prado read like a roll-call of Madrid's most popular attractions. Temples to high culture include the Museo del Prado, Museo Thyssen-Bornemisza and Centro de Arte Reina Sofía, which rank among the world's most prestigious art galleries. Up the hill to the east, the marvellous Parque del Buen Retiro helps to make this one of the most attractive areas of Madrid in which to spend your time.

The Paseo del Prado, a former river and now one of Europe's grandest boulevards, is all about the fabulous art galleries arrayed along or close to its shores. With other grand monuments and the city's botanical gardens also in residence, it's very much a daytime neighbourhood, one that all but shuts down – at least by Madrid standards – after dark. Metro stations sit at either end of the Paseo del Prado with none in between – when walking from one end to the other, take the footpaths under the trees down the centre of the Paseo, not those on the outer extremities. The barrio (district) of Huertas climbs up the hill to the west.

Getting There

Ⓜ Banco de España metro station (line 2) to the north and Atocha station (line 1) to the south sit at either end of the Paseo del Prado. For the Parque del Buen Retiro, the most convenient station is Retiro (line 2); Ibiza (line 9) also leaves you in a good place, but it isn't as well connected to the centre.

Neighbourhood Map on p102

Palacio de Comunicaciones (p103), Plaza de la Cibeles
BRIAN KINNEY/SHUTTERSTOCK ©

Top Sight 📷
Museo del Prado

◎ MAP P102, B4

Welcome to one of the world's premier art galleries. The Museo del Prado's collection is like a window onto the historical vagaries of the Spanish soul, at once grand and imperious in the royal paintings of Velázquez, darkly tumultuous in Goya's Pinturas negras (Black Paintings) *and outward looking with sophisticated works of art from all across Europe.*

www.museodelprado.es

Paseo del Prado

adult/child €15/free, 6-8pm Mon-Sat & 5-7pm Sun free, audio guide €3.50, admission plus official guidebook €24

⏱10am-8pm Mon-Sat, to 7pm Sun

Ⓜ Banco de España

Goya

Francisco Goya is sometimes described as the first of the great Spanish masters and his work is found on all three floors of the Prado. Begin at the southern end of the ground or lower level where, in Rooms 64 and 65, Goya's *El dos de mayo* and *El tres de mayo* rank among Madrid's most emblematic paintings. In the adjacent rooms (66 and 67), his disturbing *Pinturas negras* (Black Paintings) are so named for the distorted animalesque appearance of their characters. The *Saturno devorando a su hijo* (Saturn Devouring His Son) is utterly unsettling, while *La romería de San Isidro* and *Aquelarre* or *El gran cabrón* (The Great He-Goat) are dominated by the compelling individual faces of the condemned souls. An interesting footnote to *Pinturas negras* is *El coloso,* a Goyaesque work hanging next to the *Pinturas negras* that was long considered part of the master's portfolio until the Prado's experts decided otherwise in 2008.

Up on the 1st floor, other masterful works include the intriguing *La família de Carlos IV,* which portrays the Spanish royal family in 1800; Goya portrayed himself in the background just as Velázquez did in *Las meninas.* Also present are *La maja vestida* (The Young Lady Dressed) and *La maja desnuda* (The Young Lady Undressed). These portraits of an unknown woman, commonly believed to be the Duquesa de Alba (who some think may have been Goya's lover), are identical save for the lack of clothing in the latter.

Velázquez

Velázquez's role as court painter means that his works provide a fascinating insight into 17th-century royal life and the Prado holds the richest collection of his works. Of all the works by Velázquez, *Las meninas* (The Maids of Honour; Room 12) is what most people come to see.

★ Top Tips

o Plan to make a couple of visits; the Prado can be overwhelming if you try to absorb it all at once.

o A single-day ticket costs €15. A two-day pass costs €22.

o Buy your tickets online in advance to avoid the queues.

✖ Take a Break

Tucked away a block or two west of the Paseo del Prado, Los Gatos (p75) is a fabulous Madrid tapas bar and its irreverent decor is the perfect antidote to all that high-minded art.

Completed in 1656, it is more properly known as *La família de Felipe IV* (The Family of Felipe IV). It depicts Velázquez himself on the left and, in the centre, the infant Margarita. There's more to it than that: the artist in fact portrays himself painting the king and queen, whose images appear, according to some experts, in mirrors behind Velázquez. His mastery of light and colour is never more apparent than here. An interesting detail of the painting, aside from the extraordinary cheek of painting himself in royal company, is the presence of the cross of the Order of Santiago on his vest. The artist was apparently obsessed with being given a noble title. He received it shortly before his death, but in this oil painting he has awarded himself

the order years before it would in fact be his.

The rooms surrounding *Las meninas* (Rooms 14 and 15) contain more fine paintings of various members of royalty who seem to spring off the canvas, many of them on horseback. Also nearby is his *La rendición de Breda* (The Surrender of Breda), while other Spanish painters worth tracking down in the neighbouring rooms include Bartolomé Esteban Murillo, José de Ribera and the stark figures of Francisco de Zurbarán.

The Flemish Collection

The Prado's outstanding collection of Flemish art includes the fulsome figures and bulbous cherubs of Peter Paul Rubens (1577–1640). His signature works are *Las tres gracias* and *Adoración de los reyes magos*.

Las meninas by Velázquez

The Life & Times of Goya

Francisco José de Goya y Lucientes (1746–1828) started his career as a cartoonist in Madrid's Royal Tapestry Workshop. In 1792 illness left him deaf; many critics speculate that his condition was largely responsible for his wild, often merciless style that would become increasingly unshackled from convention. By 1799 Goya was appointed Carlos IV's court painter.

After painting his enigmatic masterpieces *La maja vestida* and *La maja desnuda*, and the frescoes in Madrid's Ermita de San Antonio de la Florida, the arrival of the French and war in 1808 had a profound impact on Goya; *El dos de mayo* and, more dramatically, *El tres de mayo* are unforgiving portrayals of the brutality of war.

After he retired to the Quinta del Sordo (Deaf Man's House), west of the Río Manzanares in Madrid, he created his nightmarish *Pinturas negras* (Black Paintings). Executed on the walls of the house, they were later removed and now hang in the Museo del Prado. Goya spent the last years of his life in voluntary exile in France, where he continued to paint until his death.

Other fine works in the vicinity include *The Triumph of Death* by Pieter Bruegel and those by Anton Van Dyck.

Van Der Weyden's 1435 painting *El descendimiento* is unusual, both for its size and for the recurring crossbow shapes in the painting's upper corners, which are echoed in the bodies of Mary and Christ (the painting was commissioned by a Crossbow Manufacturers Brotherhood). Once the central part of a triptych, the painting is filled with drama and luminous colours.

On no account miss the weird and wonderful *The Garden of Earthly Delights* (Room 56A) by Hieronymus Bosch (c 1450–1516). No one has yet been able to provide a definitive explanation for this hallucinatory work, although many have tried. The closer you look, the harder it is to escape the feeling that he must have been doing some extraordinary drugs.

Judith at the Banquet of Holofernes, the only painting by Rembrandt in the Prado's collection, was completed in 1634; note the artist's signature and date on the the arm of the chair. The painting shows a master at the peak of his powers, with an expert use of the chiaroscuro style, and the astonishing detail in the subject's clothing and face.

El Greco

This Greek-born artist (hence the name) is considered the finest of the Prado's Spanish Renaissance painters. The vivid, almost surreal works by this 16th-century master and adopted Spaniard, whose figures are characteristically slender and tortured, are perfectly executed. Two of his more than 30 paintings in the collection – *The Annunciation* and *The Flight into Egypt* – were painted in Italy before the artist arrived in Spain, while *The Trinity* and *Knight with His Hand on His Breast* are considered his most important works.

Emperor Carlos V on Horseback (Titian)

Considered one of the finest equestrian and royal portraits in art history, this 16th-century work is said to be the forerunner to similar paintings by Diego Rodríguez de Silva Velázquez a century later. One of the great masters of the Renaissance, Titian (1488–1576) was entering his most celebrated period as a painter when he created this, and it is widely recognised as one of his masterpieces.

The Best of the Rest

No matter how long you spend in the Prado, there's always more to discover, such as the paintings by Dürer, Rafael, Tintoretto, Sorolla, Gainsborough, Fra Angelico, Tiepolo...

Edificio Villanueva

The Prado's western wing (Edificio Villanueva) was completed in 1785 as the neoclassical Palacio de Villanueva. It served as a cavalry barracks for Napoleon's troops between 1808 and 1813. In 1814 King Fernando VII decided to use the palace as a museum. Five years later the Museo del Prado opened with 311 Spanish paintings on display.

Edificio Jerónimos

The Prado's eastern wing (Edificio Jerónimos) is part of the Prado's stunning modern extension. Dedicated to temporary exhibitions (usually to display Prado masterpieces held in storage for decades for lack of wall space), its main attraction is the 2nd-floor cloisters. Built in 1672 with local granite, the cloisters were until recently attached to the adjacent **Iglesia de San Jerónimo El Real** (91 420 35 78; Calle de Ruiz de Alarcón; admission free; 10am-1pm & 5-8.30pm; Atocha, Banco de España).

Casón del Buen Retiro

This **building** (902 107077; Calle de Alfonso XII 28; hours vary; Retiro) overlooking the Parque del Buen Retiro is run as an academic library by the nearby Museo del Prado. The Prado runs guided visits to the stunning Hall of the Ambassadors, which is crowned by the astonishing 1697 ceiling fresco *The Apotheosis of the Spanish Monarchy* by Luca Giordano.

Museo del Prado

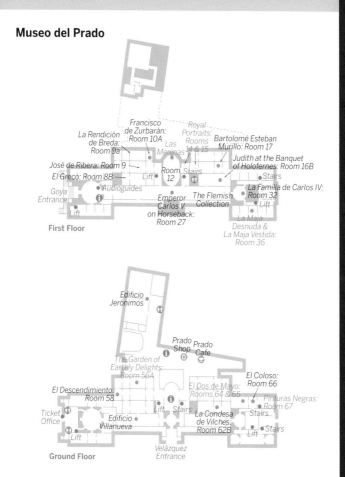

First Floor

La Rendición de Breda: Room 9a

Francisco de Zurbarán: Room 10A

Royal Portraits: Rooms 14 & 15

Bartolomé Esteban Murillo: Room 17

Judith at the Banquet of Holofernes: Room 16B

José de Ribera: Room 9

Las Meninas

El Greco: Room 8B

Room 12

Stairs

Stairs

Goya Entrance

Audioguides

Lift

La Familia de Carlos IV: Room 32

Lift

Emperor Carlos V on Horseback: Room 27

The Flemish Collection

La Maja Desnuda & La Maja Vestida: Room 36

Ground Floor

Edificio Jerónimos

Prado Shop

Prado Cafe

The Garden of Earthly Delights: Room 56A

El Descendimiento: Room 58

El Dos de Mayo: Rooms 64 & 65

El Coloso: Room 66

Pinturas Negras: Room 67

Ticket Office

Edificio Villanueva

Lift

Stairs

La Condesa de Vilches: Room 62B

Stairs

Lift

Stairs

Lift

Velázquez Entrance

Top Sight 📷
Museo Thyssen-Bornemisza

One of the most extraordinary collections of pre-dominantly European art in the world, the Museo Thyssen-Bornemisza is a worthy member of Madrid's 'Golden Triangle' of art. Where the Prado or Reina Sofía enable you to study the work of a particular artist in depth, the Thyssen is a place to immerse yourself in a breathtaking breadth of artistic styles.

◉ MAP P102, A3

☏ 902 760511

www.museothyssen.org

Paseo del Prado 8

adult/child €12/free, Mon free

🕑 10am-7pm Tue-Sun, noon-4pm Mon

Ⓜ Banco de España

Religious Art

The 2nd floor, which is home to medieval art, includes some real gems hidden among the mostly 13th- and 14th-century and predominantly Italian, German and Flemish religious paintings and triptychs. Much of it is sacred art that won't appeal to everyone, but it somehow captures the essence of medieval Europe.

Rooms 5 & 10

Unless you have a specialist's eye for the paintings that fill the first four rooms, pause for the first time in Room 5, still on the 2nd floor, where you'll find one work by Italy's Piero della Francesca (1410–92) and the instantly recognisable *Portrait of King Henry VIII* by Holbein the Younger (1497–1543). In Room 8, *Jesus Among the Doctors* by Albrecht Dürer, a leading figure in the German Renaissance, is an exceptional, vaguely disturbing work; note Dürer's anagram on the slip of paper emerging from the book in the painting's foreground. Continue on to Room 10 for the evocative 1586 *Massacre of the Innocents* by Lucas Van Valckenborch.

Spain & Venice

Room 11 is dedicated to El Greco (with three pieces) and his Venetian contemporaries Tintoretto and Titian, while Caravaggio and the Spaniard José de Ribera dominate Room 12. A single painting each by Murillo and Zurbarán add further Spanish flavour in the two rooms that follow, while the exceptionally rendered views of Venice by Canaletto (1697–1768) should on no account be missed. Few paintings have come to be the iconic image of a city quite like Canaletto's *View of Piazza San Marco* – the painter's use of line and angle, and the intense detail in even the smallest of the painting's figures give a powerful sense of atmosphere and movement.

The Baroness Collection I

Best of all on the top floor is the extension (Rooms A to H), which houses the collection of

★ **Top Tips**

o The excellent audioguide allows you to zero in on particular paintings, which counters the feeling of being overwhelmed by such a wide-ranging collection.

o Unlike many Madrid museums, the Thyssen opens on a Monday and is free, but crowds can be large. For smaller crowds (but you'll have to pay), arrive as soon as they open any other day.

✕ **Take a Break**

o Estado Puro (p104), just around the roundabout within sight of the museum entrance, is this sophisticated and relentlessly creative tapas bar.

For a casual sit-down meal it's hard to ignore Maceiras (p74), the purveyors of fine Galician cooking just up the hill in Huertas in the Paseo del Prado hinterland.

El Retiro & the Art Museums Museo Thyssen-Bornemisza

Carmen Thyssen-Bornemisza; the rest belonged to Baron Thyssen-Bornemisza, a German-Hungarian magnate and her late husband. Room C houses paintings by Canaletto, Constable and Van Gogh, while the stunning Room H includes works by Monet, Sisley, Renoir, Pissarro and Degas.

Rooms 28 to 35

The 1st floor is where the Thyssen really shines. There's a Gainsborough in Room 28 and a Goya in Room 31. The latter's *Asensio Julià* is believed to be dedicated to Goya's friend and fellow artist, the eponymous Valencian painter who worked with Goya on the frescoes in the Ermita de San Antonio de la Florida (p138). Also in Room 31, one of the Thyssen's lesser-known masterpieces, the 19th-century *Dresden Easter Morning* by Caspar David Friedrich, is a haunting study in light and texture by one of the leading figures in the German Romantic movement. The painting is rich in symbolism – the moon and dawn evoke death and resurrection – and the shades of colour portray shifts of extraordinary subtlety.

If you've been skimming the surface, Room 32 is the place to linger over every painting. The astonishing texture of Van Gogh's *Les Vessenots* is a masterpiece, but the same applies to Manet's *Woman in Riding Habit,* Monet's *The Thaw at Vétheuil,* Renoir's *Woman with a Parasol in a Garden* and Pissarro's *Rue Saint-Honoré in the Afternoon.* Simply extraordinary.

There's no time to catch your breath, because Room 33 is similarly something special with Cézanne, Gauguin, Toulouse-Lautrec and Degas all on show. The big names continue in Room 34 (Picasso, Matisse and Modigliani) and 35 (Edvard Munch and Egon Schiele).

The Baroness Collection II

In the 1st floor's extension (Rooms I to P), Room K has works by Monet, Pissarro, Sorolla and Sisley, while Room L is the domain of Gauguin (including his iconic *Mata Mua*), Degas and Toulouse-Lautrec. Rooms M (Munch), N (Kandinsky), O (Matisse and Georges Braque) and P (Picasso, Matisse, Edward Hopper and Juan Gris) round out an outrageously rich journey.

Cubism & Surrealism

Down on the ground floor, in Room 41 you'll see a nice mix of the big three of cubism – Picasso, Georges Braque and Madrid's own Juan Gris – along with several other contemporaries. Wassily Kandinsky is the main drawcard in Room 43, while there's an early Salvador Dalí alongside Max Ernst and Paul Klee in Room 44.

20th-Century Icons

Pablo Picasso appears in Room 45, another of the gallery's standout rooms; it includes works by Marc Chagall and Dalí. Room 46 has Joan Miró's *Catalan Peasant with a Guitar,* Jackson Pollock's *Brown and Silver I* and the deceptively simple but strangely pleasing *Untitled (Green on Maroon)* by Mark Rothko.

Museo Thyssen-Bornemizsa

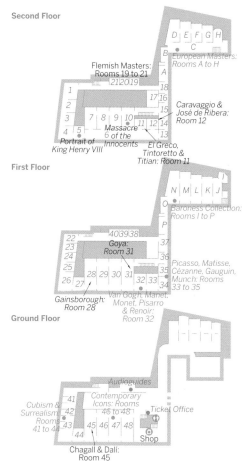

Second Floor

D E F G H
C
B
A
European Masters:
Rooms A to H

Flemish Masters:
Rooms 19 to 21
21 20 19
18
1
17 16
2
15
Caravaggio &
3
José de Ribera:
7 8 9 10 11 12 14
Room 12
Massacre
4 5
6 of the
13
Portrait of
Innocents
El Greco,
King Henry VIII
Tintoretto &
Titian: Room 11

First Floor

I
N M L K J
O
Baroness Collection:
Rooms I to P
P

22
40 39 38
23
Goya:
24
Room 31
37
25
36
28 29 30 31
35
Picasso, Matisse,
26 27
32 33
Cézanne, Gauguin,
34
Munch: Rooms
Gainsborough:
Van Gogh, Manet,
33 to 35
Room 28
Monet, Pisarro
& Renoir:
Ground Floor
Room 32

Audioguides

Contemporary
41
Icons: Rooms
Cubism &
42
46 to 48
Ticket Office
Surrealism:
43
Rooms
45 46 47 48
41 to 44
44
Shop
Chagall & Dalí:
Room 45

Top Sight 📷
Centro de Arte Reina Sofía

Home to Picasso's Guernica, arguably Spain's single-most famous artwork, and a host of other important Spanish artists, the Centro de Arte Reina Sofía is Madrid's premier collection of contemporary art. In addition to plenty of paintings by Picasso, other major drawcards are works by Salvador Dalí and Joan Miró. The collection spans the 20th century up to the 1980s.

◎ **MAP P102, A6**

www.museoreinasofia.es
Calle de Santa Isabel 52
adult/concession €10/free,
1.30-7pm Sun, 7-9pm Mon
& Wed-Sat free, tickets
cheaper online
🕙10am-9pm Mon & Wed-
Sat, to 7pm Sun
Ⓜ Atocha

Picasso's Guernica

Claimed by some to be the most important artwork of the 20th century, Pablo Picasso's *Guernica* (1937) measures 3.5m by 7.8m and is an icon of the cubist style for which Picasso became famous. You could easily spend hours studying the painting; take the time to both examine the detail of its various constituent elements and step back to gain an overview of this extraordinary canvas.

To deepen your understanding of *Guernica*, don't neglect the sketches that Picasso painted as he prepared to execute his masterpiece. They're in the rooms surrounding Room 206. They offer an intriguing insight into the development of this seminal work.

Other Cubist Masters

Picasso may have been the brainchild behind the cubist form, but he was soon joined by others who saw its potential. Picasso is said to have been influenced by the mask traditions of Africa, and these elements can also be discerned in the work of Madrid-born Juan Gris (1887–1927) or Georges Braque (1882–1963), two of the masters of the genre.

Joan Miró

The work of Joan Miró (1893–1983) is defined by often delightfully bright primary colours. After his paintings became a symbol of the Barcelona Olympics in 1992, his work began to receive the international acclaim it so richly deserved and the museum is a fine place to view a representative sample of his innovative style.

★ Top Tips

o The permanent collection is on the 2nd and 4th floors of the museum's main wing, the Edificio Sabatini.

o *Guernica's* location (Room 206, 2nd floor) never changes.

o The Reina Sofía's paintings are grouped together by theme rather than artist – pick up a copy of the Planos de Museo (Museum Floorplans).

✗ Take a Break

Visible from the museum's entrance, **El Brillante** (☑ 91 528 69 66; Plaza del Emperador Carlos V; bocadillos €4.50-7, raciones €7.50-13; ⊙ 7.30am-2.30am Sep-Jul; Ⓜ Atocha) is a breezy, no-frills bar-eatery.

Not far west of the gallery, **La Buga del Lobo** (☑ 91 528 88 38; www.facebook. com/labugadellobo; Calle de Argumosa 11; mains €12-20; ⊙ 11am-2am Wed-Mon; Ⓜ Lavapiés) is a funky bar-restaurant, as good for a drink as a meal.

Picasso's Guernica

Guernica is one of the most famous paintings in the world, a signature work of cubism whose disfiguration of the human form would become an eloquent symbol of a world's outrage at the horrors wrought upon the innocent by modern warfare. For some it's an overtly political work, a moment captured in time when the world lost its innocence. For others it is the painting that announced the arrival of an entirely new genre, of which it remains the most enduring symbol.

After the Spanish Civil War broke out in 1936, Picasso was commissioned by the Republican government of Madrid to do the painting for the Paris Exposition Universelle in 1937. As news filtered out about the bombing of Gernika (Guernica) in the Basque Country by Hitler's Legión Condor at the request of Franco, Picasso committed his anger to canvas. At least 200 people (possibly many more) died in the 26 April 1937 attack and much of the town was destroyed. To understand the painting's earth-shattering impact at the time, it must be remembered that the attack on Guernica represented the first use of airborne military hardware to devastating effect, and served as a precursor to the devastation wrought by weapons of mass destruction in WWII.

Guernica has always been a controversial work and was initially derided by many as being more propaganda than art – Picasso was no friend of Franco's and he would spend much of his later life in exile. The painting subsequently migrated to the USA, where it spent time in numerous museums across the country. It only returned to Spain in 1981, in keeping with Picasso's wish that the painting return to Spanish shores only once democracy had been restored.

Given the subject matter, the Basques believe that its true home is in the Basque Country and calls to have it moved there continue unabated. Such a move is, however, unlikely to happen any time soon, with the Reina Sofía arguing that the painting is too fragile to be moved again.

Salvador Dalí

The Reina Sofía is home to around 20 canvases by Salvador Dalí, of which the most famous is perhaps the surrealist extravaganza *El gran masturbador* (1929); at once disturbing and utterly compelling, this is one of the museum's standout paintings. Look also for a strange bust of a certain *Joelle* done by Dalí and his friend Man Ray.

Contemporary Spanish Artists

The Reina Sofía offers a terrific opportunity to learn more about lesser-known 20th-century Spanish artists. Among these are: Miquel Barceló (b 1957); *madrileño* artist José Gutiérrez Solana (1886–1945); the renowned Basque painter Ignacio Zuloaga (1870–1945); and Benjamín Palencia (1894–1980), whose paintings capture the turbulence of Spain in the 1930s.

The late Barcelona painter Antoni Tàpies (1923–2012), for years one of Spain's most creative talents, is represented, as are the pop art of Eduardo Arroyo (b 1937), abstract painters such as Eusebio Sempere (1923–85) and members of the Equipo 57 group (founded in 1957 by a group of Spanish artists in exile in Paris), including Pablo Palazuelo (1916–2007).

Sculptures

Of the sculptors, watch for Pablo Gargallo (1881–1934), whose work in bronze includes a bust of Picasso, and the renowned Basque sculptors Jorge Oteiza (1908–2003) and Eduardo Chillida (1924–2002); Chillida's forms rendered in rusted wrought iron are among Spanish art's most intriguing forms.

Edificio Nouvel

Beyond its artwork, the Reina Sofía is an important architectural landmark, adapted from the shell of an 18th-century hospital with eye-catching external glass lifts. The stunning extension (the Edificio Nouvel), which spreads along the western tip of the Plaza del Emperador Carlos V, hosts temporary exhibitions, auditoriums, the bookshop, a cafe and the museum's library.

Top Sight 📷
Parque del Buen Retiro

The glorious gardens of El Retiro are as beautiful as any you'll find in a European city. Littered with marble monuments, landscaped lawns, the occasional elegant building and abundant greenery, it's quiet and contemplative during the week but comes to life on weekends. Put simply, this is one of our favourite places in Madrid.

◎ **MAP P102, C3**

Plaza de la Independencia

🕑 6am-midnight May-Sep, to 10pm Oct-Apr

Ⓜ Retiro, Príncipe de Vergara, Ibiza, Atocha

Lake (El Estanque)

The focal point for so much of El Retiro's life is the artificial *estanque* (lake), which is watched over by the massive ornamental structure of the **Monument to Alfonso XII** on the east side, complete with marble lions. On the southern end of the lake, the odd structure decorated with sphinxes is the **Fuente Egipcia** (Egyptian Fountain; ⏰6am-midnight May-Sep, to 10pm Oct-Apr): legend has it that an enormous fortune buried in the park by Felipe IV in the mid-18th century rests here. Just down the hill and south of the lake, the sober 1883 **Palacio de Velázquez** (www.museoreinasofia.es; admission varies; ⏰10am-10pm May-Sep, to 7pm Oct, to 6pm Nov-Apr) is used for temporary exhibitions organised by the Centro de Arte Reina Sofía.

Palacio de Cristal

Hidden among the trees south of the lake is the **Palacio de Cristal** (📞91 574 66 14; www.museoreinasofia.es; ⏰10am-10pm Apr-Sep, to 7pm Oct, to 6pm Nov-Mar), a magnificent metal-and-glass structure that is arguably El Retiro's most beautiful architectural monument. It was built in 1887 as a winter garden for exotic flowers and is now used for temporary exhibitions organised by the Centro de Arte Reina Sofía (p96).

Ermita de San Isidro

In the northeastern corner of El Retiro, the small country chapel is the **Ermita de San Isidro** (Paseo del Quince de Mayo 62), among the few, albeit modest, examples of extant Romanesque architecture in Madrid. Parts of the wall, a side entrance and part of the apse were restored in 1999 and are all that remain of the 13th-century building. When it was built Madrid was a little village more than 2km away.

Just south of the Ermita de San Isidro, amid sculpted hedgerows and wandering peacocks, is **La Casa de Fieras**, Madrid's former zoo, which was once home to the same camels that played a starring role in *Lawrence of Arabia*.

★ Top Tips

○ If you're going to rent a boat on the weekend, do so around 3pm to 4pm when most locals are having lunch.

○ Kiosks sell pricey drinks and there are cafes around the park, but little food is for sale – we recommend packing a picnic instead.

✗ Take a Break

Ideal for a picnic lunch, but also a pleasant cafe in its own right, Mallorca (p116) is a fine pit stop en route to or from the park.

Viridiana (p104) is one of Madrid's most enduring and creative top-end restaurants. It's open for lunch and dinner but advance bookings are highly recommended.

El Retiro & the Art Museums

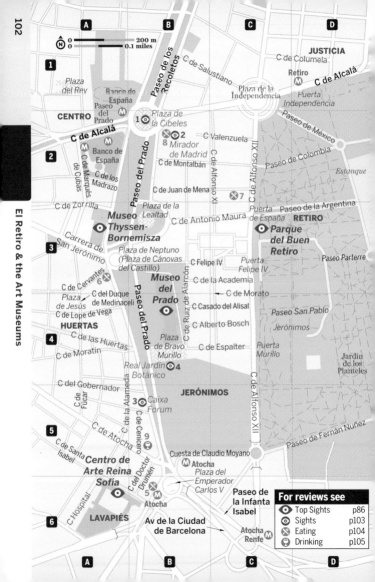

CENTRO

Plaza del Rey

Banco de España

Paseo del Prado

C de Alcalá

Banco de España

C de Marqués de Cubas

C de los Madrazo

C de Zorrilla

Carrera de San Jerónimo

C de Cervantes

Plaza de Jesús

C del Duque de Medinaceli

C de Lope de Vega

HUERTAS

C de las Huertas

C de Moratín

C del Gobernador

C de Fúcar

C de la Alameda

C de Atocha

C de Cenicero

C del Doctor Drumén

C de Santa Isabel

C Hospital

LAVAPIÉS

Centro de Arte Reina Sofía ⓞ

Paseo de los Recoletos

C de Salustiano

Plaza de la Cibeles

Plaza de la Independencia

JUSTICIA

C de Columela

Retiro Ⓜ

C de Alcalá

Puerta Independencia

Paseo de México

Mirador de Madrid

C Valenzuela

C de Montalbán

C de Juan de Mena

Paseo de Colombia

Paseo del Prado

C de Antonio Maura

Plaza de la Lealtad

Museo Thyssen-Bornemisza ⓞ

Plaza de Neptuno (Plaza de Cánovas del Castillo)

Museo del Prado ⓞ

Plaza de Bravo Murillo

Real Jardín Botánico ⓞ

CaixaForum ⓞ

Paseo del Prado

C de Ruiz de Alarcón

C Felipe IV

C de la Academia

C de Morato

C Casado del Alisal

C Alberto Bosch

C de Espalter

C de Alfonso XII

C de Alfonso XI

Puerta de España

Paseo de la Argentina

RETIRO

Parque del Buen Retiro ⓞ

Estanque

Paseo Parterre

Puerta Felipe IV

Paseo San Pablo

Jerónimos

Puerta Murillo

Jardín de los Planteles

JERÓNIMOS

Paseo de Fernán Nuñez

Cuesta de Claudio Moyano

Atocha Ⓜ
Plaza del Emperador Carlos V

Atocha

Paseo de la Infanta Isabel

Atocha Renfe

Av de la Ciudad de Barcelona

0 ─── 200 m
0 ─── 0.1 miles

For reviews see

ⓞ	Top Sights	p86
⊙	Sights	p103
✕	Eating	p104
⊖	Drinking	p105

Sights

Plaza de la Cibeles SQUARE

1 ⊙ MAP P102, B2

Of all the grand roundabouts that punctuate the Paseo del Prado, Plaza de la Cibeles most evokes the splendour of imperial Madrid. The jewel in the crown is the astonishing **Palacio de Comunicaciones** (☎91 480 00 08; www.centrocentro.org; Plaza de la Cibeles 1; admission free; ⏰10am-8pm Tue-Sun; Ⓜ Plaza de España). Other landmark buildings around the plaza's perimeter include the **Palacio de Linares and Casa de América** (☎91 595 48 00, ticket reservations 902 221424; www.casamerica.es; Plaza de la Cibeles 2; adult/student & senior/child €8/5/free; ⏰guided tours 11am, noon & 1pm Sat & Sun Sep-Jul, shorter hours Aug, ticket office 10am-3pm & 4-8pm Mon-Fri; Ⓜ Banco de España), the **Palacio Buenavista** (Plaza de la Cibeles; Ⓜ Banco de España) and the national **Banco de España** (Calle de Alcalá 48). The spectacular fountain of the goddess Cybele at the centre of the plaza is one of Madrid's most beautiful. (Ⓜ Banco de España)

Mirador de Madrid VIEWPOINT

2 ⊙ MAP P102, B2

The views from the summit of the Palacio de Comunicaciones are among Madrid's best, sweeping out over Plaza de la Cibeles, up the hill towards the sublime Edificio Metrópolis and out to the mountains. Buy your ticket up the stairs then take the lift to the 6th floor, from where the gates are opened every half hour. You can either take another lift or climb the stairs up to the 8th floor. (www.centrocentro.org; 8th fl, Palacio de Comunicaciones, Plaza de la Cibeles; adult/child €2/0.50; ⏰10.30am-1.30pm & 4-7pm Tue-Sun; Ⓜ Banco de España)

Caixa Forum MUSEUM, ARCHITECTURE

3 ⊙ MAP P102, B5

This extraordinary structure is one of Madrid's most eye-catching landmarks. Seeming to hover above the ground, the brick edifice is topped by an intriguing summit of rusted iron. On an adjacent wall is the *jardín colgante* (hanging garden), a lush (if thinning) vertical wall of greenery almost four storeys high. Inside there are four floors of exhibition space awash in stainless steel and with soaring ceilings. The exhibitions here are always worth checking out and include photography, contemporary painting and multimedia shows. (☎91 330 73 00; https://obrasociallacaixa.org/en/cultura/caixaforum-madrid/que-hacemos; Paseo del Prado 36; adult/child €4/free; ⏰10am-8pm; Ⓜ Atocha)

Real Jardín Botánico GARDENS

4 ⊙ MAP P102, B5

Madrid's botanical gardens are a leafy oasis in the centre of town, though they're not as expansive or as popular as the Parque del Buen

Retiro. With some 30,000 species crammed into a relatively small 8-hectare area, it's more a place to wander at leisure than laze under a tree, although there are benches dotted throughout the gardens where you can sit.

In the centre stands a statue of Carlos III, who in 1781 moved the gardens here from their original location at El Huerto de Migas Calientes, on the banks of the Río Manzanares, while the **Pabellón Villanueva**, on the eastern flank of the gardens, frequently stages art exhibitions – the opening hours are the same as for the park and the exhibitions are usually free.There are Spanish-language **guided visits** to the gardens; reservations by phone are essential. (Royal Botanical Garden; 🖉91 420 04 38; www.rjb.csic.es; Plaza de Bravo Murillo 2; adult/child €4/ free; ⏱10am-9pm May-Aug, to 8pm Apr & Sep, to 7pm Mar & Oct, to 6pm Nov-Feb; Ⓜ Atocha)

Eating

El Brillante   SPANISH €

5 ⊗ MAP P102, B6

Just by the Centro de Arte Reina Sofía, this breezy, no-frills bar-eatery is a Madrid institution for its bocadillos (filled rolls) – the bocadillo de cala-mares has been a favourite for more than half a century – and no-nonsense raciones (large tapas servings). It's also famous for serving chocolate con churros or porras (chocolate

with deep-fried doughnuts) in the wee hours after a hard night on the tiles. (🖉91 528 69 66; Plaza del Emperador Carlos V; bocadillos €4.50-7, raciones €7.50-13; ⏱7.30am-2.30am Sep-Jul; Ⓜ Atocha)

Estado Puro   TAPAS €€

6 ⊗ MAP P102, A3

A slick but casual tapas bar, Estado Puro serves up fantastic tapas, such as the *tortilla española siglo XXI* (21st-century Spanish omelette, served in a glass…), quail eggs in soy sauce or pig's trotters with cuttlefish noodles. The kitchen is overseen by Paco Roncero, head chef at La Terraza del Casino (p75), who learned his trade with master chef Ferran Adrià. (🖉91 330 24 00; www.tapas enestadopuro.com; Plaza de Neptuno/ Plaza de Cánovas del Castillo 4; tapas €4.50-12.50, mains €14-20; ⏱noon-midnight; Ⓜ Banco de España, Atocha)

Viridiana   MODERN SPANISH €€€

7 ⊗ MAP P102, C2

Chef Abraham García is a much-celebrated Madrid figure and his larger-than-life personality is reflected in Viridiana's menu. Many influences are brought to bear on the cooking here, among them international innovations and in-gredients and well-considered sea-sonal variations. (🖉91 523 44 78; www.restauranteviridiana.com; Calle de Juan de Mena 14; mains €28-39, menú de degustación €100; ⏱1.30-4pm & 8pm-midnight; Ⓜ Banco de España)

Tapas from Estado Puro

Palacio de Cibeles   SPANISH €€€

8 🍴 MAP P102, B2

High in the iconic Palacio de Comunicaciones on Plaza de la Cibeles (see 1 ◎ Map p102, B2), this much-loved restaurant by Adolfo Muñoz takes Spanish staples, gives them a twist from the Castilla-La Mancha region, and then riffs a little wherever the urge takes him. (☏91 523 14 54; www.palaciodecibeles.com; 6th fl, Plaza de la Cibeles 1; mains €16-39, set menus €38.50-55; ⏱1-4pm & 8pm-midnight; Ⓜ Banco de España)

Drinking

Teatro Kapital   CLUB

9 🍺 MAP P102, B5

One of the most famous mega-clubs in Madrid, this seven-storey venue has something for everyone, from cocktail bars and dance music to karaoke, salsa, hip hop, chilled spaces and an open-air rooftop. There's even a 'Kissing Room'. Door staff have their share of altitude and don't mind refusing entrance if you give them any lip. (☏91 420 29 06; www.grupo-kapital.com; Calle de Atocha 125; admission from €17; ⏱midnight-6am Thu-Sat; Ⓜ Atocha)

Explore ◈
Salamanca

The barrio (district) of Salamanca is Madrid's most exclusive quarter. Like nowhere else in the capital, this is where stately mansions set back from the street share barrio space with big local and international designer boutiques. Salamanca's sprinkling of fine restaurants, designer tapas bars and niche museums are also very much at home here.

One of the larger barrios that we cover, Salamanca can look daunting on a map, but it's easily navigated for the most part on foot. Calle de Serrano and Calle de José Ortega y Gasset are the two main shopping strips, and if you're in town to shop then there's very little of interest that's more than a short detour from these two main axes.

Although you will find bars and nightclubs here, Salamanca is very much a daytime barrio. Salamanca's tapas bars and restaurants overflow with a busy lunchtime crowd during the week when eating is often a pit stop on part of a shopping itinerary. We suggest you do likewise to really get under Salamanca's skin. By evening, things are much quieter, with many people coming specifically to eat before heading elsewhere in Madrid to continue their night.

Getting There

Ⓜ Serrano and Velázquez (both line 4) or Núñez de Balboa (lines 4 and 5) are the most convenient metro stations; the last means a downhill walk to most of the barrio. Gregorio Marañon (lines 7 and 10) is best for the Museo Lázaro Galdiano. Ventas (lines 2 and 5) is the station for the Plaza de Toros.

Neighbourhood Map on p112

Shopping on Calle de Serrano ALEX SEGRE/ALAMY STOCK PHOTO ©

Top Sight 📷
Museo Lázaro Galdiano

This imposing early-20th-century Italianate stone mansion, set discreetly back from the street, belonged to Don José Lázaro Galdiano, a successful businessman and passionate patron of the arts. His astonishing private collection, which he bequeathed to the city upon his death, contains 13,000 works of art and objets d'art (including paintings by some of Europe's grand masters), a quarter of which are on show at any time.

◉ **MAP P112, B2**

☏ 91 561 60 84

www.flg.es

Calle de Serrano 122

adult/concession/child €6/3/free, last hour free

🕙 10am-4.30pm Tue-Sat, to 3pm Sun

Ⓜ Gregorio Marañón

Checklist of Old Masters

It can be difficult to believe the breadth of masterpieces that Galdiano gathered during his lifetime, and there's enough here to merit this museum's inclusion among Madrid's best art galleries. The highlights include works by Francisco de Zurbarán, Claudio Coello, Hieronymus Bosch, Bartolomé Esteban Murillo, El Greco, Lucas Cranach and John Constable, and there's even a painting in Room 11 attributed to Diego Rodríguez de Silva Velázquez.

Goya

As is often the case, Goya belongs in a class of his own. He dominates Room 13, while the ceiling of the adjoining Room 14 features a collage from some of his more famous works. Some that are easy to recognise include *La maja desnuda, La maja vestida* and the frescoes of the Ermita de San Antonio de la Florida (p138).

Curio Collection

This remarkable collection ranges beyond paintings to sculptures, bronzes, miniature figures, jewellery, ceramics, furniture, weapons...clearly Galdiano was a man of wide interests. The ground floor is largely given over to a display setting the social context in which he lived, with hundreds of curios from all around the world on show. There are more on the top floor.

Frescoes & Textiles

The lovely 1st floor, which contains many of the Spanish artworks, is arrayed around the centrepiece of the former ballroom and beneath lavishly frescoed ceilings. On no account miss the top floor's Room 24, which contains some exquisite textiles.

★ Top Tips

o The museum is a long uphill walk from the rest of Salamanca – take the metro here and walk back down.

o Unless you have a specialist interest, the guides on sale at the entrance are unnecessary – English and Spanish labelling is excellent.

o Seek out the photos of each room to see how it appeared in Galdiano's prime.

✖ Take a Break

Across the road from the museum, José Luis (p116) is where the young and wealthy come to sip bottled mineral water and order *tortilla de patatas* (Spanish potato omelette).

Astrolabius (p115), also nearby, has a playful approach to traditional Spanish ingredients and is a lovely place to eat or pause with over a drink and tapas at the bar.

Walking Tour 🚶

Shopping in Upmarket Salamanca

*From international designers with no need for
introductions to Spanish household names that
the shopper in you will adore discovering, Salamanca is a fashionista's dream come true. Add
some terrific gourmet food purveyors and casual
but classy pit stops along the way and it's a day to
remember if shopping gets you excited.*

Walk Facts

Start Camper; **M** Serrano

End El Lateral;
M Velázquez, Núñez de
Balboa

Length 2.5km; two to four
hours

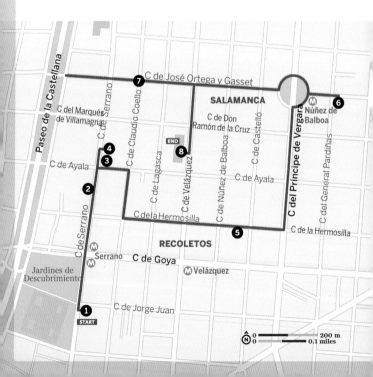

❶ Camper

Spanish fashion is not all haute couture. **Camper** (☎ 91 578 25 60; www.camper.com; Calle de Serrano 24; ◷ 10am-9pm Mon-Sat, noon-8pm Sun; Ⓜ Serrano), the world-famous cool and quirky shoe brand from Mallorca, offers bowling-shoe chic with colourful, fun designs that couple quality with comfort.

❷ Agatha Ruiz de la Prada

Agatha Ruiz de la Prada (☎ 91 319 05 01; www.agatharuizdelaprada. com; Calle de Serrano 27; ◷ 10am-8.30pm Mon-Sat; Ⓜ Serrano) has to be seen to be believed, with pinks, yellows and oranges everywhere you turn. It's fun and exuberant, but not just for kids. It also has serious and highly original fashion.

❸ Bombonerías Santa

When locals want a tasteful gift to take to their next dinner party, many of them come to Bombonerías Santa (p119). The exquisitely presented chocolates here are reason enough to join them, dinner party or not.

❹ Manolo Blahnik

The world-famous shoe designer **Manolo Blahnik** (☎ 91 575 96 48; www.manoloblahnik.com; Calle de Serrano 58; ◷ 10am-2pm & 4-8pm Mon-Sat; Ⓜ Serrano) has a boutique along Calle de Serrano. The showroom is exclusive and each shoe is displayed like a work of art.

❺ Restaurante Estay

Backtracking slightly away to the southeast, Restaurante Estay (p117) is partly a Spanish bar, where besuited waiters serve *café con leche*, and also one of the best-loved tapas bars in this part of town. There's a long list of tapas and it's a classy but casual place to rest before continuing.

❻ Oriol Balaguer

Catalan pastry chef Oriol Balaguer (p119) won a prize for the World's Best Dessert in 2001. More recently, his croissants won the title of Spain's best in 2014. His chocolate boutique is like a small art gallery dedicated to exquisite, finely crafted chocolate collections and cakes.

❼ Calle de José Ortega y Gasset

The world's most prestigious international designers occupy what is known as *la milla del oro* (the golden mile) along Calle de José Ortega y Gasset, close to the corner with Calle de Serrano. On the south side of the street, there's Giorgio Armani and Chanel. Just across the road is Louis Vuitton and Cartier. And that's just the start...

❽ El Lateral

This chic **wine bar** (☎ 91 435 06 04; www.lateral.com; Calle de Velázquez 57; tapas €1.55-9.80, raciones €7-13; ◷ noon-1am Sun-Wed, to 2am Thu-Sat; Ⓜ Velázquez, Núñez de Balboa) is cool in the right places, filled as it is with slick suits and classic wines alongside the new wave of style shaking up the *barrio*. It's a classic perch along one of Salamanca's main boulevards to wind down after a hard day's shopping.

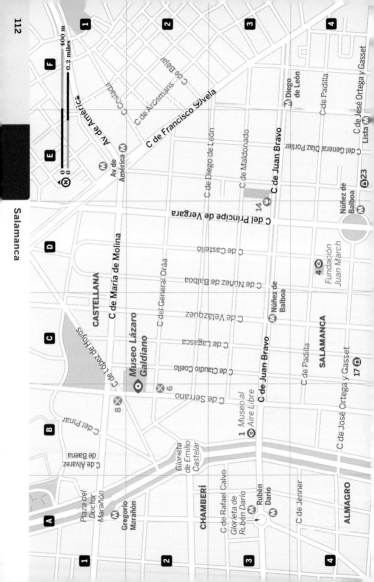

400 m
0.2 miles

A **B** **C** **D** **E** **F**

Av de América

C de Castañal
C de Arcamans
C de Belar

C de Francisco Silvela

Plaza del Doctor Marañón
C del Pinar
C de Álvarez de Baena

Gregorio Marañón Ⓜ

CASTELLANA
C de María de Molina

C del López de Hoyos

Ⓜ Av de América

C de Diego de León
C de Maldonado
C del Principe de Vergara

Ⓜ Diego de León
C de Padilla
C de José Ortega y Gasset

Museo Lázaro Galdiano ●

Ⓧ 8

C del General Oráa

C de Serrano
Ⓧ 6

Glorieta de Emilio Castelar

CHAMBERÍ
C de Rafael Calvo
Glorieta de Rubén Darío

Rubén Darío Ⓜ

1 Museo al Aire Libre ●

C de Claudio Coello
C de Lagasca
C de Castelló
C de Núñez de Balboa
C de Velázquez

Ⓜ Núñez de Balboa

C de Juan Bravo

C de Padilla
C de José Ortega y Gasset

SALAMANCA

4 ● Fundación Juan March

14 Ⓧ

C de Juan Bravo

C del General Díaz Portier

Núñez de Balboa Ⓜ

Ⓜ Lista

C de José Ortega y Gasset

Ⓐ 23
17 Ⓐ

ALMAGRO
C de Jenner

Salamanca

5
6
7
8
5
6
7
8

C de Alcatara

C de Don Ramón de la Cruz

C del Conde de Peñalver

GOYA

Goya Ⓜ

Plaza de
Salvador
Dalí

C de Ayala

C de la Hermosilla

C del General Pardiñas

C de Goya

Goya Ⓜ

C de Narváez

15 Ⓘ

C de Alcalá

C del Duque de Sesto

C del Príncipe de Vergara

C del General
Díaz Porlier

C de O'Donnell

Ⓔ

Ⓕ

For reviews see

◉ Top Sights   p108
Ⓘ Sights   p114
✕ Eating   p115
✕ Drinking   p117
Ⓢ Shopping   p118

C de Jorge Juan

Príncipe
de Vergara Ⓜ

Av de Menéndez Pelayo

C de Castelló

24 ✕

10 ✕ Ⓘ

12 ✕

C de Núñez de Balboa

Velázquez Ⓜ

19 Ⓢ

Paseo del Duque
de Fernán Núñez

Ⓓ

C del Marqués de Villamagna

C de Villanueva

RECOLETOS

C de Ayala

16 Ⓘ

18 Ⓘ

**Mercado
de la Paz**

C de la Hermosilla

C de Goya

C de Velázquez

13 Ⓘ

C de Villanueva

Parque
del Buen
Retiro

Ⓒ

21 Ⓘ

22 Ⓘ

Serrano Ⓜ

7 ✕

C de Serrano

C de Claudio Coello

C de Jorge Juan

C del Conde de Aranda

JUSTICIA

5 ◉ Lab Room Spa

11 ✕

C de Columela

C de Alcalá

Ⓑ

C de Zurbarán

C de Fernando
el Santo

Colón Ⓜ

**Jardines de
Descubrimiento**

**Biblioteca
Nacional &
Museo del Libro**

3 Ⓘ

20 Ⓘ

9 ✕

**Museo
Arqueológico
Nacional**

2 ◉

C de Villanueva

Retiro Ⓜ

C del Cid

C de los Recoletos

C de Salustiano

Plaza de la
Independencia

Ⓐ

Paseo de los Recoletos

Paseo de la Castellana

5
6
7
8

Sights

Museo al Aire Libre
SCULPTURE

1 ◉ MAP P112, B3

This fascinating open-air collection of 17 abstract sculptures includes works by renowned Basque artist Eduardo Chillida, Catalan master Joan Miró, as well as Eusebio Sempere and Alberto Sánchez, among Spain's foremost sculptors of the 20th century. The sculptures are beneath the overpass where Paseo de Eduardo Dato crosses Paseo de la Castellana, but somehow the hint of traffic grime and pigeon shit only adds to the appeal. All but one are on the eastern side of Paseo de la Castellana. (Paseo de la Castellana; admission free; ⏰24hr; Ⓜ Rubén Darío)

Museo Arqueológico Nacional
MUSEUM

2 ◉ MAP P112, B7

The showpiece National Archaeology Museum contains a sweeping accumulation of artefacts behind its towering facade. Daringly redesigned within, the museum ranges across Spain's ancient history and the large collection includes stunning mosaics taken from Roman villas across Spain, intricate Muslim-era and Mudéjar handiwork, sculpted figures such as the *Dama de Ibiza* and *Dama de Elche*, examples of Romanesque and Gothic architectural styles and a partial copy of the prehistoric cave paintings of Altamira (Cantabria).

Mercado de la Paz
🍽

One of few Madrid markets to have been gentrified in recent years, **Mercado de la Paz** (Map p112, C5; 📞91 435 07 43; www.mercadolapaz.es; off Calle de Ayala; ⏰9am-2.30pm & 5-8pm Mon-Fri, 9am-2.30pm Sat; Ⓜ Serrano) remains a thoroughly local market. Fresh produce, meat and fish are the mainstays, but there's plenty of things to buy and eat as you go (cured meats and cheeses, for example).

(📞91 577 79 12; www.man.es; Calle de Serrano 13; admission €3, 2-8pm Sat & 9.30am-noon Sun free; ⏰9.30am-8pm Tue-Sat, to 3pm Sun; Ⓜ Serrano)

Biblioteca Nacional & Museo del Libro
LIBRARY, MUSEUM

3 ◉ MAP P112, A7

Perhaps the most impressive of the grand edifices erected along the Paseo de los Recoletos in the 19th century, the 1892 Biblioteca Nacional (National Library) dominates the southern end of Plaza de Colón. Downstairs, and entered via a separate entrance, the fascinating museum is a must for bibliophiles, with interactive displays on printing presses and other materials, illuminated manuscripts, the history of the library, and literary cafes. (📞91 580 78 05; www.bne.es; Paseo de los Recoletos

20; admission free; ⊙library 9am-9pm Mon-Fri, to 2pm Sat mid-Sep–mid-Jun, 9am-7.30pm Mon-Fri mid-Jun–mid-Sep, museum 10am-8pm Tue-Sat, to 2pm Sun; Ⓜ Colón)

Fundación Juan March

CULTURAL CENTRE

4 ◉ MAP P112, D4

This foundation organises some of the better temporary exhibitions in Madrid each year and it's always worth checking its website to see what's on or around the corner. It also stages concerts across a range of musical genres and other events throughout the year. (☎91 435 42 40; www.march. es; Calle de Castelló 77; admission free; ⊙11am-8pm Mon-Sat, 10am-2pm Sun & holidays; Ⓜ Núñez de Balboa)

Lab Room Spa

SPA

5 ◉ MAP P112, B8

An exclusive spa and beauty parlour whose past clients include Penélope Cruz, Jennifer Lopez, Gwyneth Paltrow and Gael García Bernal, the Lab Room is close to the ultimate in pampering for both men and women. It offers a range of make-up sessions, massages and facial and body treatments; prices can be surprisingly reasonable. (☎91 431 21 98; www. thelabroom.com; Calle de Claudio Coello 13; ⊙11am-8pm Mon-Fri, to 7pm Sat; Ⓜ Retiro)

Eating

Astrolabius

FUSION €€

6 🍴 MAP P112, B2

This terrific family-run place in Salamanca's north has a simple philosophy – take grandmother's recipes and filter them through the imagination of the grandchildren. The result is a beguiling mix of flavours, such as scallops of the world in garlic, or the prawn croquettes. The atmosphere is edgy and modern, but casual in the best Madrid sense. (☎91 562 06 11; www.astrolabiusmadrid.com; Calle de Serrano 118; mains €10-25; ⊙1-4pm & 8.30pm-midnight Tue-Sat, closed Aug; Ⓜ Núñez de Balboa)

Platea

SPANISH €€

7 🍴 MAP P112, B6

The ornate Carlos III cinema opposite the Plaza de Colón has been artfully transformed into a dynamic culinary scene with more than a hint of burlesque. There are 12 restaurants, three gourmet food stores and cocktail bars. (☎91 577 00 25; www.plateamadrid.com; Calle de Goya 5-7; ⊙12.30pm-12.30am Sun-Wed, to 2.30am Thu-Sat; Ⓜ Serrano, Colón)

Plan for a Picnic

Mallorca (p116) has some fantastic takeaway foods, and they're ideal if you're planning a picnic in the Parque del Buen Retiro, which borders Salamanca to the south.

Pollie Watch 👍

María Luisa Banzo, the owner of La Cocina de María Luisa, was formerly a prominent figure in the government of conservative Popular Party Prime Minister José María Aznar. Keep an eye out for the former PM (also from Castilla y León) and other prominent politicians in her restaurant.

José Luis
SPANISH €€

8 ⊗ MAP P112, B1

With numerous branches around Madrid, José Luis is famous for its fidelity to traditional Spanish recipes. It wins many people's vote for Madrid's best *tortilla de patatas* (Spanish potato omelette), but it's also good for *croquetas* and *ensaladilla rusa* (Russian salad). This outpost has a slightly stuffy, young-men-in-suits feel to it, which is, after all, *very* Salamanca. (☎91 563 09 58; www.joseluis.es; Calle de Serrano 89; tapas from €5; ⊙8.30am-1am Mon-Fri, 9am-1am Sat, 12.30pm-1am Sun; Ⓜ Gregorio Marañón)

Biotza
TAPAS, BASQUE €€

9 ⊗ MAP P112, B7

This breezy Basque tapas bar is one of the best places in Madrid to sample the creativity of bite-sized *pintxos* (Basque tapas) as only the Basques can make them. It's the perfect combination of San Sebastián–style tapas, Madrid-style pale-green/red-black decoration and unusual angular benches. The prices quickly add up, but it's highly recommended nonetheless. (☎91 781 03 13; Calle de Claudio Coello 27; pintxos €2.80-3.40, raciones from €6, set menus from €18; ⊙1-4.30pm & 8.30pm-midnight Mon-Sat; Ⓜ Serrano)

La Cocina de María Luisa
CASTILIAN €€€

10 ⊗ MAP P112, D7

The home kitchen of former parliamentarian María Luisa Banzo has one of Salamanca's most loyal followings. The cooking is a carefully charted culinary journey through Castilla y León, accompanied by well-chosen regional wines and rustic decor that add much warmth to this welcoming place. The house speciality comes from María Luisa's mother – pig's trotters filled with meat and black truffles from Soria. (☎91 781 01 80; www.lacocinademaria luisa.es; Calle de Jorge Juan 42; mains €18-27; ⊙1.30-4pm & 9pm-midnight Mon-Sat Sep-Jul; Ⓜ Velázquez)

Mallorca
BAKERY €

11 ⊗ MAP P112, B8

For fine takeaway food, head to Mallorca, a Madrid institution. Everything here, from gourmet mains to snacks and sweets, is delicious. (☎91 577 18 59; www.pasteleria-mallorca.com; Calle de Serrano 6; mains €7-12; ⊙9am-9pm; Ⓜ Retiro)

Restaurante Estay

TAPAS €€

12 MAP P112, D6

Restaurante Estay is partly a standard Spanish bar, where besuited waiters serve *café con leche,* and also one of the best-loved tapas bars in this part of town. The long list of hot and cold tapas concentrates mostly on Spanish staples, with a handful of more adventurous combinations. It also does breakfasts. (91 578 04 70; www.estayrestaurante.com; Calle de Hermosilla 46; tapas €1.90-4.40, 6-tapas set menu from €15; 8am-midnight Mon-Thu, to 1.30am Fri, 9am-1.30am Sat; Velázquez)

Drinking

Gabana 1800

CLUB

13 MAP P112, C7

With its upmarket crowd that invariably includes a few *famosos* (famous people), Gabana 1800 is very Salamanca. That this place has lasted the distance where others haven't owes much to the fabulous array of drinks, rotating cast of first-class DJs and fairly discerning door policy – dress to impress. (91 575 18 46; www.gabana.es; Calle Velázquez 6; admission €15; midnight-5.30am Wed-Sat; Retiro)

Platea (p115)

Almonte
CLUB

14 MAP P112, D3

If flamenco has captured your soul, but you're keen to do more than watch, head to Almonte. Live acts kick off the night, paying homage to the flamenco roots of Almonte in Andalucía's deep south. The young and the beautiful who come here have *sevillanas* (a flamenco dance style) in their soul and in their feet. (☎91 563 25 04; www.almontesalaro ciera.com; Calle de Juan Bravo 35; ⏰11pm-5am Sun-Fri, 10pm-6am Sat; M Núñez de Balboa, Diego de León)

Geographic Club
BAR

15 MAP P112, E7

With its elaborate stained-glass windows, ethno-chic from all over the world and laid-back atmosphere, the Geographic Club is an excellent choice in Salamanca for an early-evening drink – try one of the 30-plus tropical cocktails. We like the table built around an old hot-air-balloon basket almost as much as the cavern-like pub downstairs. (☎91 578 08 62; www. thegeographicclub.es; Calle de Alcalá 141; ⏰1pm-2am Sun-Thu, to 3am Fri & Sat; M Goya)

Shopping

Mantequería Bravo
FOOD & DRINKS

16 MAP P112, B5

Behind the attractive old facade lies a connoisseur's paradise, filled with local cheeses, sausages, wines and coffees. The products here are great for a gift, but everything's so good that you won't want to share. Not that long ago, Mantequería Bravo won the prize for Madrid's best gourmet food shop or delicatessen. (☎91 575 80 72; www.bravo1931.com; Calle de Ayala 24; ⏰9.30am-2.30pm & 5.30-8.30pm Mon-Fri, 9.30am-2.30pm Sat; M Serrano)

Balenciaga
FASHION & ACCESSORIES

17 MAP P112, C4

Flagship store for the celebrated Basque Balenciaga brand, with a stunning limestone-and-marble interior. (☎91 419 99 00; www. balenciaga.com; Calle de Lagasca 75; ⏰10.30am-8pm Mon-Sat; M Núñez de Balboa)

Isolée
FOOD, FASHION

18 MAP P112, B5

Multipurpose lifestyle stores were late in coming to Madrid, but they're now all the rage and there's none more stylish than Isolée, which has outlasted them all. It sells a select range of everything from clothes and shoes to CDs and food. (☎902 876136; www.isolee.com; Calle de Claudio Coello 55; ⏰11am-8.30pm Mon-Fri, to 9pm Sat; M Serrano)

Ekseption & Eks
FASHION & ACCESSORIES

19 MAP P112, C6

This elegant showroom store consistently leads the way with the latest trends, spanning catwalk designs alongside a look that is more informal, though always sophisticated. The unifying theme is urban chic and its list of designer brands includes Balenciaga, Givenchy, Marc Jacobs and Dries van Noten. (91 361 97 76; www.ekseption.es; Calle de Velázquez 28; ⏰10.30am-2.30pm & 4.30-8.30pm Mon-Sat; Velázquez)

Purificación García

FASHION & ACCESSORIES

20 MAP P112, B6

Fashions may come and go but Puri consistently manages to keep ahead of the pack. Her signature style for men and women is elegant and mature designs that are just as at home in the workplace as at a wedding. (91 435 80 13; www.purificaciongarcia.com; Calle de Serrano 28; ⏰10am-8.30pm Mon-Sat; Serrano)

De Viaje

BOOKS

21 MAP P112, B5

Whether you're after a guidebook, a coffee-table tome or travel literature, De Viaje, Madrid's largest travel bookshop, probably has it. Covering every region of the world, it has mostly Spanish titles, but some in English as well. Staff are helpful, and there's also a travel agency. (91 577 98 99; www.deviaje.com; Calle de Serrano 41; ⏰10am-8.30pm Mon-Fri, 10.30am-2.30pm & 5-8pm Sat; Serrano)

Bombonerías Santa

FOOD & DRINKS

22 MAP P112, B5

If your style is as refined as your palate, the exquisite chocolates

in this tiny shop will satisfy. The packaging is every bit as pretty as the *bombones* (chocolates) within, but they're not cheap – count on paying around €60 per kilo of chocolate. (91 576 76 25; www.bombonerias-santa.com; Calle de Serrano 56; ⏰10am-2pm & 5-8.30pm Mon, 10am-8.30pm Tue-Sat, shorter hours Jul & Aug; Serrano)

Oriol Balaguer

FOOD

23 MAP P112, E4

Catalan pastry chef Oriol Balaguer has a formidable CV – he's worked in the kitchens of Ferran Adrià in Catalonia, won the prize for the World's Best Dessert (the 'Seven Textures of Chocolate'). His chocolate boutique is presented like a small art gallery dedicated to exquisite chocolate collections and cakes.(91 401 64 63; www.oriolbalaguer.com; Calle de José Ortega y Gasset 44; ⏰9am-8.30pm Mon-Fri, 10am-8.30pm Sat, 10am-2.30pm Sun; Núñez de Balboa)

Cuarto de Juegos

TOYS

24 MAP P112, D7

We're not sure if it's an official rule, but batteries seem to be outlawed at this traditional toy shop, where all kinds of old-fashioned board games and puzzles are still sold. Yes, there's Ludo, Chinese checkers and backgammon, but there's so much more here and they're not just for kids. (91 435 00 99; www.cuartodejuegos.es; Calle de Jorge Juan 42; ⏰10am-8.30pm Mon-Fri, 10.30am-2pm & 5-8pm Sat; Velázquez, Príncipe de Vergara)

Worth a Trip 🔭
Plaza de Toros & Museo Taurino

Madrid's Plaza de Toros Monumental de Las Ventas (Las Ventas) is the heart and soul of Spain's bullfighting tradition and the most prestigious bullring in the world. A visit here is a good way to gain an insight into this very Spanish tradition, but the architecture also makes it worth visiting for those with no interest in la corridas (bullfights).

📞 91 356 22 00
www.las-ventas.com
Calle de Alcalá 237
admission free
🕙 10am-5.30pm
Ⓜ Ventas

Architecture

One of the largest rings in the bullfighting world, Las Ventas can hold 25,000 spectators, and has a grand Mudéjar (a Moorish architectural style) exterior and a suitably coliseum-like arena surrounding the broad sandy ring.

Puerta de Madrid

The grand and decidedly Moorish Puerta de Madrid symbolises the aspiration of all bull-fighters and, suitably, it's known colloquially as the 'gate of glory'. Madrid's bullfighting crowd is known as the most demanding in Spain – if they carry a *torero* (bullfighter) out through the gate (usually clutching an ear or a tail – other trophies awarded to an elite few), it's because he has performed exceptionally.

Guided Tours

Although you can visit the ring without taking a tour, we strongly recommend that you take one of the **guided visits** (☏ 687 739032; www.lasventastour.com; adult/child €13/10; ⏱ 10am-5.30pm, days of bullfight 10am-1.30pm; Ⓜ Ventas), which take you out onto the sand and into the royal box. Tours are in English and Spanish and must be booked in advance.

Museo Taurino

The **Museo Taurino** (☏ 91 725 18 57; www.las-ventas.com; Calle de Alcalá 237; admission free; ⏱ 10am-5.30pm; Ⓜ Ventas) inhabits a newly renovated space dedicated to bullfighting legend Manolete, as well as a curious collection of paraphernalia, costumes (the *traje de luces*, or suit of lights, is one of bullfighting's most recognisable props), photos and other bullfighting memorabilia up on the top floor above one of the two courtyards by the ring. It's a fascinating insight into the whole subculture that surrounds bullfighting.

★ Top Tips

○ Even if you can't bear to imagine attending a bullfight, it's worth visiting to admire the architecture and to inform yourself about the traditions that lie behind bullfighting.

○ If you take the tour, ask questions – the guides are well-informed and, in our experience, willing to engage in a discussion about bullfighting's more unpleasant aspects.

✕ Take a Break

One of Madrid's most soul-stirring events, the singing of La Salve Rociera at **El Rincón de Jerez** www.elnuevorincon dejerez.es; Calle de Rufino Blanco 5; raciones €7-15; ⏱ 1-4.30pm & 7pm-midnight Tue-Sun Sep-Jul; Ⓜ Manuel Bacerra) is an evening-only affair, but it's otherwise a handy lunch pit stop.

It's a fair walk back down towards Salamanca, but it's mostly downhill and Geographic Club (p118) is a perfect place to stop for a drink.

Explore

Malasaña & Chueca

The two inner-city barrios (districts) of Malasaña and Chueca are where Madrid gets up close and personal. Here, it's more an experience of life as it's lived by madrileños (people from Madrid) than the traditional traveller experience of ticking off from a list of wonderful, if more static, attractions. These are barrios with attitude and personality, where Madrid's famed nightlife, shopping and eating choices live and breathe and take you under the skin of the city.

Malasaña and Chueca are at their best in the evening and into the night – other than a flurry of activity around lunchtime as people hurry to and from their favourite tapas bar or restaurant, these barrios mostly live for the night.

Calle de Fuencarral is the dividing line between the two, a narrow but nonetheless major city thoroughfare that has been pedestrianised for much of its length. If Malasaña holds fast to its roots, Chueca wears its heart on its sleeve, a barrio that the gay and lesbian community has transformed into one of the coolest places in Spain. Sometimes it's in your face, but more often it's what locals like to call 'hetero-friendly'.

Getting There

Ⓜ Chueca metro station (line 5) sits right in the heart of Chueca, while Tribunal (lines 1 and 10) serves a similar purpose in Malasaña. Noviciado (lines 2 and 10) is good for Conde Duque. Other convenient metro stations around the perimeters of these neighbourhoods include San Bernardo, Bilbao, Alonso Martínez, Gran Vía and Santo Domingo.

Neighbourhood Map on p126

Bar facade in Malasaña JJFARQ/SHUTTERSTOCK ©

Walking Tour 🚶

Counterculture in Malasaña

Malasaña was the epicentre of la movida madrileña (the Madrid scene) in the 1900s, and that spirit lives on here. Partly it survives in retro bars, nightclubs and shops that pay homage to the '70s and '80s. But there's also a 'new' and appealing trend towards the vintage aspect of Malasaña life. The common theme is the alternative slant these places take on life in their bid to relive or re-create the past.

Walk Facts

Start Retro City;
Ⓜ Tribunal

End Plaza Dos de Mayo;
Ⓜ Tribunal

Length 1.5km; two to three hours

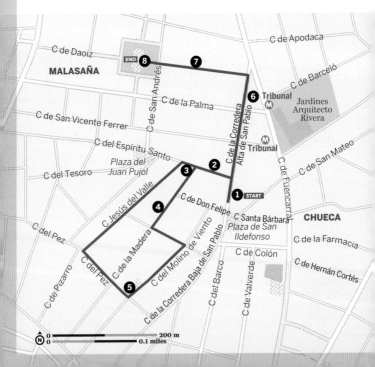

❶ Retro City

Retro City (Calle de Corredera Alta de San Pablo 4; ⏰noon-2.30pm & 5.30-9pm Mon-Sat), with its 'vintage for the masses', lives for the colourful '70s and '80s. Whereas other stores in the *barrio* have gone for an angry, thumb-your-nose-at-society look, Retro City just looks back with nostalgia.

❷ Snapo

Snapo (www.snaposhoponline.com; Calle del Espíritu Santo 6; ⏰11am-2pm & 5-8.30pm Mon-Sat; Ⓜ Tribunal) is rebellious Malasaña to its core, disrespecting the niceties of fashion respectability. It does jeans, caps and jackets, but its T-shirts are the Snapo trademark.

❸ Lolina Vintage Café

Lolina Vintage Café (www.lolina cafe.com; Calle del Espíritu Santo 9; ⏰10am-midnight Sun-Thu, to 2.30am Fri & Sat; Ⓜ Tribunal) captures the essence of the *barrio* in one small space. With a studied retro look (comfy old-style chairs and sofas, gilded mirrors and 1970s-era wallpaper).

❹ Casa Julio

A city-wide poll for Madrid's best *croquetas* (croquettes; fried rolls with filling) would see half voting for **Casa Julio** (Calle de la Madera 37; 6/12 croquetas €6/12; ⏰1-3.30pm & 6.30-11pm Mon-Sat Sep-Jul; Ⓜ Tribunal) and the remainder not doing so because they haven't voted yet. There's the traditional *jamón* (ham) variety or more creative choices.

❺ Bar Palentino

Formica tables, no attention to detail, and yet... **Bar Palentino** (Calle del Pez 8; bocadillos €2.50; ⏰7am-2pm Mon-Sat; Ⓜ Noviciado) is an ageless Malasaña bar wildly popular with young and old alike. Its irresistible charm derives from its tables, and owners María Dolores and Casto.

❻ Tupperware

A Malasaña stalwart and prime candidate for the bar that best catches the enduring *rockero* spirit of Malasaña, **Tupperware** (www. tupperwareclub.com; Calle de la Corredera Alta de San Pablo 26; ⏰9pm-3am Mon-Wed, 8pm-3.30am Thu-Sat, 8pm-3am Sun; Ⓜ Tribunal) draws a 30-something crowd, spins indie rock with a bit of soul and classics from the '60s and '70s, and generally revels in its kitsch.

❼ La Vía Láctea

A living, breathing and delightfully grungy relic of *la movida*, **La Vía Láctea** (www.facebook.com/lavia lacteabar; Calle de Velarde 18; ⏰8pm-3am Sun-Thu, to 3.30am Fri & Sat; Ⓜ Tribunal) remains a Malasaña favourite for an informal crowd that lives for the 1980s. The music ranges across rock, pop, garage, rockabilly and indie.

❽ Plaza Dos de Mayo

By day it's the preserve of dog-walkers and families, but by night the crowds spill from neighbouring bars onto the plaza to celebrate the freedom of living Madrid. Very Malasaña.

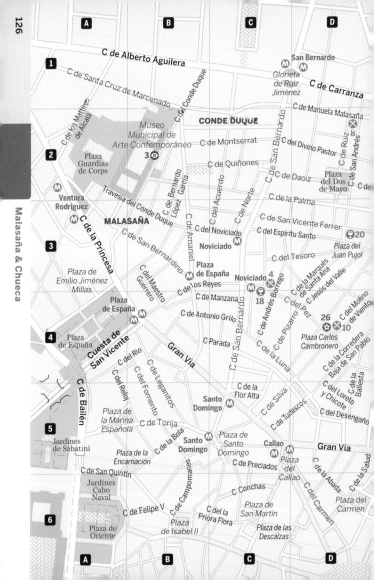

Malasaña & Chueca

A **B** **C** **D**

C de Alberto Aguilera

1 C de Santa Cruz de Marcenado

San Bernardo

Glorieta de Ruiz Jiménez

C de Carranza

C de Manuela Malasaña

C de los Mártires de Alcalá

Museo Municipal de Arte Contemporáneo

CONDE DUQUE

C del Conde Duque

C de San Bernardo

C del Divino Pastor

C de Ruiz

C de San Andrés

2 **3**

Plaza Guardias de Corps

C de Montserrat

C de Quiñones

C de Daoiz

Plaza del Dos de Mayo

Ventura Rodríguez

Travesía del Conde Duque

C de Bernardo López García

C del Acuerdo

C de Norte

C de la Palma

C de San Vicente Ferrer

20

MALASAÑA

3

C de la Princesa

C de San Bernardino

C de Amaniel

C del Noviciado

C del Espíritu Santo

C del Tesoro

Plaza del Juan Pujol

Plaza de Emilio Jiménez Millas

C del Maestro Guerrero

Noviciado

Plaza de España

C de San Bernardo

Noviciado

4

C de la Marqués de Santa Ana

C de Jesús del Valle

C de los Reyes

18

C de Andrés Borrego

C de Pizarro

C del Pez

C del Molino de Viento

Plaza de España

C de Manzana

26 **10**

4

Plaza de España

Cuesta de San Vicente

C del Río

Gran Vía

C de Antonio Grilo

C Parada

C de la Luna

Plaza Carlos Cambronero

C de la Corredera Baja de San Pablo

C de la Ballesta

C del Reloj

C del Fomento

C de Leganitos

Santo Domingo

C de la Flor Alta

C de Silva

C del Loreto y Chicote

C del Desengaño

5

C de Bailén

Jardines de Sabatini

Plaza de la Marina Española

C de Torija

C de la Bola

Santo Domingo

Plaza de Santo Domingo

C de Tudescos

Callao

Gran Vía

Plaza de la Encarnación

C de San Quintín

Plaza de Preciados

Callao

Plaza del Callao

C de la Abada

C de la Salud

6

Jardines Cabo Naval

C de Felipe V

C de Campomanes

Plaza de Isabel II

C de la Priora Flora

C Conchas

Plaza de San Martín

C del Carmen

Plaza del Carmen

Plaza de Oriente

Plaza de las Descalzas

A **B** **C** **D**

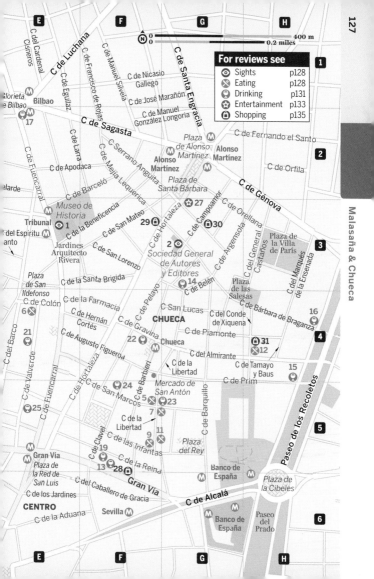

Malasaña & Chueca

For reviews see
⊙ Sights   p128
✕ Eating   p128
🍷 Drinking   p131
⭐ Entertainment p133
🛍 Shopping   p135

E **F** **G** **H**

N
0   400 m
0   0.2 miles

C del Cardenal Cisneros
C de Luchana
C de Eguilaz
Glorieta de Bilbao
Bilbao
17
C de Francisco de Rojas
C de Manuel Silvela
C de Nicasio Gallego
C de José Marañón
C de Santa Engracia
C de Manuel González Longoria
C de Fernando el Santo
C de Sagasta
C de Larra
C de Fuencarral
C de Apodaca
C de Mejía Lequerica
C Serrano Anguita
Plaza de Alonso Martínez
Alonso Martínez
Alonso Martínez
C de Orfila
Plaza de Santa Bárbara
C de Génova
Plaza de la Villa de París
elarde
C de Barceló
Museo de Historia
1
Tribunal
del Espíritu anto
C de la Beneficencia
C de San Mateo
29
C de Hortaleza
C de Campoamor
27
30
C de Oreliana
C del General Castaños
C de Argensola
C del Marqués de la Ensenada
Jardines Arquitecto Rivera
C de San Lorenzo
2
Sociedad General de Autores y Editores
Plaza de la Villa de París
Plaza de San Ildefonso
C de la Santa Brígida
C de Colón
6
C de la Farmacia
C de Hernán Cortés
C de Pelayo
14
C de Belén
Plaza de las Salesas
C de Bárbara de Braganza
16
21
CHUECA
C San Lucas
C del Conde de Xiquena
C de Augusto Figueroa
C de Gravina
22
Chueca
C de Piamonte
31
12
C del Almirante
15
C de Tamayo y Baus
C de Prim
C del Barco
C de Valverde
C de Fuencarral
25
C de Hortaleza
24
C de San Marcos
C de Barbieri
C de la Libertad
Mercado de San Antón
5
23
C de la Libertad
C de Clavel
9
11
Plaza del Rey
C de las Infantas
C de Barquillo
Gran Vía
Plaza de la Red de San Luis
19
13
28
C de la Reina
Gran Vía
Banco de España
Plaza de la Cibeles
C de los Jardines
C del Caballero de Gracia
CENTRO
C de la Aduana
Sevilla
C de Alcalá
Banco de España
Paseo del Prado
Paseo de los Recoletos

E **F** **G** **H**

1
2
3
4
5
6

Sights

Museo de Historia
MUSEUM

1 🎯 MAP P126, E3

The fine Museo de Historia (formerly the Museo Municipal) has an elaborate and restored baroque entrance, raised in 1721 by Pedro de Ribera. Behind this facade, the collection is dominated by paintings and other memorabilia charting the historical evolution of Madrid. The highlights are Goya's *Allegory of the City of Madrid* (on the 1st floor); the caricatures lampooning Napoleon and the early-19th-century French occupation of Madrid (1st floor); and the expansive model of Madrid as it was in 1830 (basement). (🕿 91 701 16 86; www.madrid.es/museodehistoria; Calle de Fuencarral 78; admission free; 🕙 10am-8pm Tue-Sun; 🇲 Tribunal)

Sociedad General de Autores y Editores
ARCHITECTURE

2 🎯 MAP P126, G3

This swirling, melting wedding cake of a building is as close as Madrid comes to the work of Antoni Gaudí, which so illuminates Barcelona. It's a joyously self-indulgent ode to Modernisme (an architectural and artistic style, influenced by art nouveau and sometimes known as Catalan modernism) and is virtually one of a kind in Madrid. Casual visitors are actively discouraged, but what you see from the street is impressive enough. The only exceptions are on the first Monday of October, International Architecture Day, when its interior staircase alone is reason enough to come and look inside. (General Society of Authors & Editors; Calle de Fernando VI 4; 🇲 Alonso Martínez)

Museo Municipal de Arte Contemporáneo
MUSEUM

3 🎯 MAP P126, B2

This rich collection of modern Spanish art includes mostly paintings and graphic art with a smattering of photography, sculpture and drawings. Highlights include Eduardo Arroyo and Basque sculptor Jorge Oteiza. Running throughout the collection are creative interpretations of Madrid's cityscape – avant-garde splodges and almost old-fashioned visions of modern Madrid side by side, among them a typically fantastical representation of the Cibeles fountain by one-time icon of *la movida madrileña* (the Madrid scene), Ouka Leele. (🕿 91 588 59 28; www.madrid.es/museoartecontemporaneo; Calle del Conde Duque 9-11; admission free; 🕙 10am-2pm & 5.30-8.30pm Tue-Sat, 10.30am-2pm Sun; 🇲 Ventura Rodríguez)

Eating

Pez Tortilla
TAPAS €

4 🍴 MAP P126, C3

Every time we come here, this place is full to bursting, which is not surprising given its philosophy of great tortilla (15 kinds!), splendid

Mercado de San Antón 🍽

Spain's fresh food markets make for an interesting alternative to bars and restaurants. Many have been transformed to meet all of your food needs at once. Downstairs at **Mercado de San Antón** (Map p126, F4; www.mercadosananton. com; Calle de Augo Figueroa 24; tapas from €1.50, mains €5-20; ⏰10am-midnight; Ⓜ Chueca) is all about fresh produce, but upstairs there's all manner of appealing tapas varieties from all corners of the country/globe.

croquetas (croquettes) and craft beers (more than 70 varieties, with nine on tap). The croquetas with black squid ink or the tortilla with truffle brie and jamón (ham) are two stars among many. (🕿653 919984; www.peztortilla.com; Calle del Pez 36; tapas from €4; ⏰noon-midnight Sun, 6.30pm-2am Mon-Wed, noon-2am Thu, noon-2.30am Fri & Sat; Ⓜ Noviciado)

Bazaar   MODERN SPANISH €

5 🍴 MAP P126, F5

Bazaar's popularity among the well-heeled Chueca set shows no sign of abating. Its pristine white interior design, with theatre-style lighting and wall-length windows, may draw a crowd that looks like it's stepped out of the pages of ¡Hola! magazine, but the food is extremely well priced and innovative, and the atmosphere is casual. (🕿91 523 39 05; www.restaurant bazaar.com; Calle de la Libertad 21; mains €7.50-13; ⏰1.15-4pm & 8.30-11.30pm Sun-Wed, 1.15-4pm & 8.15pm-midnight Thu-Sat; 📶; Ⓜ Chueca)

Bodega de la Ardosa   TAPAS €

6 🍴 MAP P126, E4

Going strong since 1892, the charming, wood-panelled bar of Bodega de la Ardosa is brimful with charm. To come here and not try the salmorejo (cold tomato soup made with bread, oil, garlic and vinegar), croquetas or tortilla de patatas (potato and onion omelette) would be a crime. On weekend nights there's scarcely room to move. (🕿91 521 49 79; www.laardosa.es; Calle de Colón 13; tapas & raciones €4-12; ⏰8.30am-2am Mon-Fri, 12.45pm-2.30am Sat & Sun; Ⓜ Tribunal)

La Carmencita   SPANISH €€

7 🍴 MAP P126, F5

Around since 1854, La Carmencita is the bar where legendary poet Pablo Neruda was once a regular. The folk of La Carmencita have taken 75 of their favourite traditional Spanish recipes and brought them to the table, sometimes with a little updating but more often safe in the knowledge that nothing needs changing. (🕿91 531 09 11; www.tabernalacarmencita.es; Calle de la Libertad 16; mains €13-27; ⏰9am-2am; Ⓜ Chueca)

Albur

TAPAS €€

8 ⊗ MAP P126, D2

One of Malasaña's best deals, this place has a wildly popular tapas bar and a classy but casual restaurant out the back. The restaurant waiters never seem to lose their cool, and their extremely well-priced rice dishes are the stars of the show, although in truth you could order anything here and leave well satisfied. (☎91 594 27 33; www.restaurantealbur.com; Calle de Manuela Malasaña 15; mains €13-18; ⏰12.30-5pm & 7.30pm-midnight Mon-Thu, 12.30-5pm & 7.30pm-1.30am Fri, 1pm-1.30am Sat, 1pm-midnight Sun; 🛜; Ⓜ Bilbao)

Celso y Manolo

TAPAS, SPANISH €€

9 ⊗ MAP P126, F5

One of Chueca's best bars, Celso y Manolo serves up tostadas for those looking to snack, oxtail for those looking for a touch of the traditional, and a host of dishes from Spain's north and northwest. There are also good wines, good coffee, even better cocktails and an artfully restored interior. (☎91 531 80 79; www.celsoymanolo.es; Calle de la Libertad 1; raciones €7.50-12; ⏰1-4.30pm & 8pm-2am; Ⓜ Banco de España)

La Mucca de Pez

TAPAS €€

10 ⊗ MAP P126, D4

The only problem with this place is that it's such an agreeable spot to spend an afternoon it can be impossible to snaffle a table. An ample wine list complements the great salads, creative pizzas and a good mix of meat and seafood mains, and the atmosphere simply adds to the overall appeal. (☎91 521 00 00; www.lamucca.es; Plaza Carlos Cambronero 4; mains €9-16; ⏰noon-1.30am Sun-Wed, 1pm-2am Thu, 1pm-2.30am Fri & Sat; Ⓜ Callao)

Bocaito

TAPAS €€

11 ⊗ MAP P126, F5

Film-maker Pedro Almodóvar once described this traditional bar and restaurant as 'the best antidepressant'. Forget about the sit-down restaurant (though well regarded) and jam into the bar, shoulder-to-shoulder with the casual crowd, order a few Andalucian raciones off the menu and slosh them down with some gritty red or a caña (small glass of beer). (☎91 532 12 19; www.bocaito.com; Calle de la Libertad 4-6; tapas €2.50-8, mains €11-28; ⏰1-4pm & 8.30pm-midnight Mon-Sat; Ⓜ Chueca, Sevilla)

La Buena Vida

SPANISH €€€

12 ⊗ MAP P126, H4

A cross between a Parisian bistro and an old-school upmarket Madrid restaurant, this prestigious Chueca place is popular with a well-heeled, knowledgable crowd. The menu is seasonal and leans towards classic Spanish tastes, although dishes like the red tuna sirloin with guacamole and sesame seeds suggest that the chefs are not averse to the odd playful interpretation. It's consistently one of Madrid's best. (☎91 531

31 49; www.restaurantelabuenavida.com; Calle del Conde de Xiquena 8; mains €25-28; ⏱1-4pm & 9-11.30pm Tue-Thu, 1.30-4pm & 9pm-12.30am Fri & Sat; Ⓜ Chueca, Colón)

Drinking

Museo Chicote

COCKTAIL BAR

13 🚇 MAP P126, F5

This place is a Madrid landmark, complete with its 1930s-era interior, and its founder is said to have invented more than 100 cocktails, which the likes of Ernest Hemingway, Ava Gardner, Grace Kelly, Sophia Loren and Frank Sinatra have all enjoyed at one time or another. (📞 91 532 67 37; www.grupomercadodelareina.com/en/museo-chicote-en/ Gran Vía 12; ⏱7pm-3am Mon-Thu, to 4am Fri & Sat, 4pm-1am Sun; Ⓜ Gran Vía)

Café Belén

BAR

14 🚇 MAP P126, G3

Café Belén is cool in all the right places – lounge and chill-out music, dim lighting, a great range of drinks (the mojitos are especially good) and a low-key crowd that's the height of casual sophistication. It's one of our preferred Chueca watering holes. (📞 91 308 27 47; www.elcafebelen.com; Calle de Belén 5; ⏱3.30pm-3am Tue-Thu, to 3.30am Fri & Sat, to midnight Sun; 📶; Ⓜ Chueca)

Gran Café de Gijón

CAFE

15 🚇 MAP P126, H4

This graceful old cafe has been serving coffee and meals since 1888 and has long been favoured by Madrid's literati for a drink or a meal – *all* of Spain's great 20th-century literary figures came here for coffee and *tertulias* (literary and philosophical discussions). You'll find yourself among intellectuals, conservative Franco diehards and young *madrileños* looking for a quiet drink. (📞 91 521 54 25; www.cafegijon.com; Paseo de los Recoletos 21; ⏱7am-1.30am; Ⓜ Chueca, Banco de España)

Café-Restaurante El Espejo

CAFE

16 🚇 MAP P126, H4

Once a haunt of writers and intellectuals, this architectural gem blends Modernista and art-deco styles, and its interior could well overwhelm you with all the mirrors, chandeliers and bow-tied service of another era. The atmosphere is suitably quiet and refined, although our favourite corner is the elegant glass pavilion out on Paseo de los Recoletos. (📞 91 308 23 47; Paseo de los Recoletos 31; ⏱8am-midnight; Ⓜ Colón)

Café Comercial

CAFE

17 🚇 MAP P126, E2

The city's oldest cafe has a special place in the hearts of many *madrileños*. Open for more than a century, it's still pulsing with life. Any day of the week you can enjoy a coffee or some food at one of the old marble-topped tables and feel like you're part of Madrid's literary and cultural scene. (📞 91 088 25 25;

www.cafecomercialmadrid.com; Glorieta de Bilbao 7; ⏰7.30am-midnight Mon-Fri, 8.30am-midnight Sat & Sun; 📶; Ⓜ Bilbao)

1862 Dry Bar   COCKTAIL BAR

18 🚇 MAP P126, C4

Great cocktails, muted early-20th-century decor and a refined air make this one of our favourite bars down Malasaña's southern end. Prices are reasonable, the cocktail list extensive and new cocktails appear every month. (📞609 531151; www.facebook.com/1862DryBar; Calle del Pez 27; ⏰3.30pm-2am Mon-Thu, to 2.30am Fri & Sat, to 10.30pm Sun; Ⓜ Noviciado)

Del Diego   COCKTAIL BAR

19 🚇 MAP P126, F5

Del Diego is one of the city's most celebrated cocktail bars. The decor blends old-world cafe with New York style, and it's the sort of place where the music rarely drowns out the conversation. Even with around 75 cocktails to choose from, we'd still order the signature 'El Diego' (vodka, advocaat, apricot brandy and lime). (📞91 523 31 06; www.deldiego.com; Calle de la Reina 12; ⏰7pm-3am Mon-Thu, to 3.30am Fri & Sat; Ⓜ Gran Vía)

Café Manuela   CAFE

20 🚇 MAP P126, D3

Stumbling into this graciously restored throwback to the 1950s along one of Malasaña's grittier streets is akin to discovering hidden treasure. There's a luminous quality to it when you come in out of the night and, like so many Madrid cafes, it's a surprisingly multifaceted space, serving cocktails and delicious milkshakes as well as offering board games atop the marble tables. (📞91 531 70 37; www.facebook.com/CafeManuela; Calle de San Vicente Ferrer 29; ⏰4pm-2am Sun-Thu, to 2.30am Fri & Sat; Ⓜ Tribunal)

Fábrica Maravillas   BREWERY

21 🚇 MAP P126, E4

Spain has taken its time getting behind the worldwide trend of boutique and artisan beers, but it's finally starting to happen. The finest example of this in Madrid is Fábrica Maravillas, a microbrewery known for its 'Malasaña Ale'. (📞91 521 87 53; www.fmaravillas.com; Calle de Valverde 29; ⏰6pm-midnight Mon-Wed, to 1am Thu, to 2am Fri, 12.30pm-2am Sat, 12.30pm-midnight Sun; Ⓜ Tribunal, Gran Vía)

Café Acuarela   CAFE

22 🚇 MAP P126, F4

A few steps up the hill from Plaza de Chueca, this longtime centrepiece of gay Madrid – a huge statue of a nude male angel guards the doorway – is an agreeable, dimly lit salon decorated with, among other things, religious icons. It's ideal for quiet conversation and catching the weekend buzz as people plan their forays into the more clamorous clubs in the vicinity. (📞91 522 21 43; Calle de Gravina 10; ⏰11am-2am Sun-Thu, to 3am Fri & Sat; Ⓜ Chueca)

Calle de Pez 💬

It's been years in the making, but Calle de Pez, down the lower, southern end of Malasaña has become one of the coolest local haunts in Madrid, a beguiling mix of grungy and cool. Around the corner, Calle de Corredera Baja de San Pablo, where it approaches Gran Vía, is undergoing a similar transformation.

Diurno   CAFE

23 🚇 MAP P126, G5

One of the most important hubs of *barrio* life in Chueca, this cafe (with DVD store attached) has become to modern Chueca what the grand literary cafes were to another age. It's always full with a fun local crowd relaxing amid the greenery. Well-priced meals and snacks are served if you can't bear to give up your seat. (☏ 91 522 00 09; www.grupomercadodelareina.com/ en/diurno-en; Calle de San Marcos 37; ⏰10am-1am Sun-Thu, to 2am Fri & Sat; Ⓜ Chueca)

Why Not?   CLUB

24 🚇 MAP P126, F5

Underground, narrow and packed with bodies, gay-friendly Why Not? is the sort of place where nothing's left to the imagination (the gay and straight crowd who come here are pretty amorous) and it's full nearly every night of the week. Pop and Top 40 music are the standard, and the dancing crowd is mixed but all serious about having a good time. (☏ 91 521 80 34; Calle de San Bartolomé 7; entrance €10; ⏰10.30pm-6am; Ⓜ Chueca)

Ya'sta   CLUB

25 🚇 MAP P126, E5

Going strong since 1985 and the height of *la movida madrileña* (the Madrid scene), Ya'sta is a stalwart of the Malasaña night. Everything gets a run here, from techno, psychedelic trance and electronica to indie pop. (☏ 91 521 88 33; www. yastaclub.net; Calle de Valverde 10; €10; ⏰11.45pm-6am Wed-Sat; Ⓜ Gran Vía)

Entertainment

Teatro Flamenco Madrid   FLAMENCO

26 ⭐ MAP P126, D4

This excellent new flamenco venue is a terrific deal. With a focus on quality flamenco (dance, song and guitar) rather than the more formal meal-and-floor-show package of the *tablaos* (choreographed flamenco shows), and with a mixed crowd of locals and tourists, this place generates a terrific atmosphere most nights for the hour-long show. Prices are also a notch below what you'll pay elsewhere. (☏ 91 159 20 05; www. teatroflamencomadrid.com; Calle del Pez 10; adult/student & senior/child €25/16/12; ⏰6.45pm & 8.15pm; Ⓜ Noviciado)

La Movida Madrileña

What London was to the swinging '60s and Paris to 1968, Madrid was to the 1980s. After the long, dark years of dictatorship and conservative Catholicism, the death of Franco and the advent of democracy, Spaniards, especially *madrileños* (people from Madrid), were prompted to emerge onto the streets with all the zeal of ex-convent schoolgirls. Nothing was taboo in a phenomenon known as *la movida madrileña* (literally the Madrid scene) as young *madrileños* discovered the '60s, '70s and '80s all at once. Drinking, drugs and sex suddenly were OK. All-night partying was the norm, drug taking in public was not a criminal offence (that changed in 1992) and the city howled.

What was remarkable about *la movida* was that it was presided over by Enrique Tierno Galván, an ageing former university professor who had been a leading opposition figure under Franco and was affectionately known throughout Spain as 'the old teacher'. A Socialist, he became mayor in 1979 and, for many, launched *la movida* by telling a public gathering *'a colocarse y ponerse al loro'*, which loosely translates as 'get stoned and do what's cool'. Unsurprisingly, he was Madrid's most popular mayor ever, and when he died in 1986, a million *madrileños* turned out for his funeral.

La movida was not just about rediscovering the Spanish art of *salir de copas* (going out for a drink). It was also accompanied by an explosion of creativity among the country's musicians, designers and film-makers, who were keen to shake off the shackles of the repressive Franco years. By one tally, Madrid was home to 300 rock bands and 1500 fashion designers during *la movida*. The most famous of these was film director Pedro Almodóvar. Although his later films became internationally renowned, his first films, *Pepi, Luci, Bom y otras chicas del montón* (Pepi, Luci, Bom and the Other Girls; 1980) and *Laberinto de pasiones* (Labyrinth of Passions; 1982) are where the spirit of the movement really comes alive.

At the height of *la movida* in 1981, Andy Warhol openly regretted that he could not spend the rest of his days here. In 1985, the *New York Times* anointed the Spanish capital 'the new cultural capital of the world and the place to be'. Things have quietened down a little since those heady days, but you'll only notice if you were here during the 1980s...

El Junco Jazz Club JAZZ

27 ⭐ MAP P126, G3

El Junco has established itself on the Madrid nightlife scene by appealing as much to jazz aficionados as to clubbers. Its secret is high-quality live jazz gigs from Spain and around the world, followed by DJs spinning funk, soul, nu jazz, blues and innovative groove beats. There are also jam sessions at 11pm in jazz (Tuesday) and blues (Sunday). (☎91 319 20 81; www.eljunco.com; Plaza de Santa Bárbara 10; €6-15; ⏰11pm-5.30am Tue-Thu, to 6am Fri & Sat; Ⓜ Alonso Martínez)

Shopping

Loewe FASHION & ACCESSORIES

28 🔒 MAP P126, F5

Born in 1846 in Madrid, Loewe is arguably Spain's signature line in high-end fashion and its landmark store on Gran Vía is one of the most famous and elegant stores in the capital. Classy handbags and accessories are the mainstays. Prices can be jaw-droppingly high, but it's worth stopping by, even if you don't plan to buy. (☎91 522 68 15; www.loewe.com; Gran Vía 8; ⏰10am-8.30pm Mon-Sat, 11am-8pm Sun; Ⓜ Gran Vía)

Patrimonio Comunal Olivarero FOOD

29 🔒 MAP P126, F3

For picking up some of the country's olive-oil varieties (Spain is the world's largest producer), this place is perfect. With examples of the extra-virgin variety (and nothing else) from all over Spain, you could spend ages agonising over the choices. Staff know their oil and are happy to help out. (☎91 308 05 05; www.pco.es; Calle de Mejía Lequerica 1; ⏰10am-2pm & 5-8pm Mon-Fri, 10am-2pm Sat Sep-Jun, 9am-3pm Mon-Sat Jul; Ⓜ Alonso Martínez)

Malababa FASHION & ACCESSORIES

30 🔒 MAP P126, G3

This corner of Chueca is one of Madrid's happiest hunting grounds for the style-conscious shopper who favours individual boutiques with personality above larger stores. One such place, light-filled Malababa features classy Spanish-made accessories, including jewellery, handbags, shoes, purses and belts, all beautifully displayed. (☎91 203 59 51; www.malababa.com; Calle de Santa Teresa 5; ⏰10.30am-8.30pm Mon-Thu, to 9pm Fri & Sat; Ⓜ Alonso Martínez)

Lurdes Bergada FASHION & ACCESSORIES

31 🔒 MAP P126, H4

Lurdes Bergada and Syngman Cucala, a mother-and-son designer team from Barcelona, offer classy and original men's and women's fashions using neutral colours and all-natural fibres. They've developed something of a cult following and it's difficult to leave without finding something that you just have to have. (☎91 531 99 58; www.lurdesbergada.es; Calle del Conde de Xiquena 8; ⏰10am-2.30pm & 4.30-8.30pm Mon-Sat; Ⓜ Chueca)

Walking Tour 🥾

Barrio Life in Chamberí

The generally upmarket barrio (district) of Chamberí is widely known as one of the most castizo (a difficult term to translate, its meaning lies somewhere between traditional and authentic) neighbourhoods of the capital. With its signature plaza, old-style shops and unmistakeable barrio feel, it's off the tourist trail and among the best places in Madrid to attempt to understand what makes the city tick.

Walk Facts

Start Plaza de Olavide;
Ⓜ Bilbao, Iglesia, Quevedo

End Sagaretxe; Ⓜ Iglesia

Length 5km; three to four hours

❶ Plaza de Olavide

Plaza de Olavide (Ⓜ Bilbao, Iglesia, Quevedo) is the hub of Chamberí life with its park benches, playgrounds and outdoor tables. Inside Bar Mentrida at No 3 you'll find a stirring photographic record of the plaza's history.

❷ Old-Fashioned Shopping

A charming old-world shoe store, **Calzados Cantero** (Plaza de Olavide 12; ⏱ 9.45am-2pm & 4.45-8.30pm Mon-Fri, 9.45am-2pm Sat; Ⓜ Iglesia) is famous for its rope-soled *alpargatas* (espadrilles), which start from €6. This place is a *barrio* classic.

❸ The King's Watchmaker

Relojería Santolaya (www. relojeriasantolaya.com; Calle Murillo 8; ⏱ 10am-1pm & 5-8pm Mon-Fri; Ⓜ Quevedo, Iglesia, Bilbao), an old clock repairer founded in 1867, is the official watch repairer to Spain's royalty and heritage properties. There's not much that's for sale, but stop by to admire the dying art of timepiece repairs.

❹ A Surprise Museum

One of Madrid's best-kept secrets, **Museo Sorolla** (www.mecd.gob.es/ msorolla; Paseo del General Martínez Campos 37; adult/child €3/free; ⏱ 9.30am-8pm Tue-Sat, 10am-3pm Sun; Ⓜ Iglesia, Gregorio Marañón) is dedicated to the Valencian artist Joaquín Sorolla, who immortalised the clear Mediterranean light of the Valencian coast.

❺ A Barrio Bar

Bodega de la Ardosa (Calle de Santa Engracia 70; raciones from €7.50; ⏱ 9am-3pm & 6-11.30pm Thu-Tue; Ⓜ Iglesia) is a fine old relic with an extravagantly tiled facade (complete with shrapnel holes from the Civil War).

❻ Chamberí's Missing Station

Abandoned in 1966, **Estación de Chamberí** (Andén 0; www.museo madrid.com/tag/anden-0-horario; cnr Calles de Santa Engracia & de Luchana; free; ⏱ 11am-1pm & 5-7pm Fri, 10am-2pm Sat & Sun; Ⓜ Iglesia, Bilbao) has finally reopened as a museum piece that re-creates the era of the station's inauguration in 1919.

❼ Old-Style Stationery

Opened in 1905, **Papelería Salazar** (www.papeleriasalazar.es; Calle de Luchana 7-9; ⏱ 9.30am-1.30pm & 4.30-8pm Mon-Fri, 10am-1.30pm Sat; Ⓜ Bilbao) is Madrid's oldest stationery store and a treasure trove filled with old-style Spanish bookplates, First Communion invitations and the like.

❽ Calle de Fuencarral

Calle de Fuencarral between the Glorietas de Bilbao and Quevedo is one of Madrid's iconic thoroughfares. On Sunday mornings, the street is closed to traffic.

❾ Basque Tapas

At journey's end, **Sagaretxe** (www. sagaretxe.com; Calle de Eloy Gonzalo 26; tapas €2.20, set menus €15.50-31; ⏱ noon-5pm & 7pm-midnight; Ⓜ Iglesia) is one of the best Basque *pintxos* (tapas) bars in Madrid. Simply point and your selection will be plated up for you.

Worth a Trip 🔭
Ermita de San Antonio de la Florida

This humble hermitage ranks alongside Madrid's finest art galleries. Also known as the Panteón de Goya, the chapel has frescoed ceilings as painted by Goya in 1798 on the request of Carlos IV. As such, it's one of the few places to see Goya masterworks in their original setting.

Panteón de Goya

📞 91 542 07 22

www.sanantoniodela
florida.es

Glorieta de San Antonio de la Florida 5

admission free

🕑 9.30am-8pm Tue-Sun, hours vary Jul & Aug

Ⓜ Príncipe Pío

The Miracle of St Anthony

Figures on the dome depict the miracle of St Anthony. The saint heard word from his native Lisbon that his father had been unjustly accused of murder. The saint was whisked miraculously to his hometown from northern Italy, where he tried in vain to convince the judges of his father's innocence. He then demanded that the corpse of the murder victim be placed before the judges. Goya's painting depicts the moment in which St Anthony calls on the corpse (a young man) to rise up and absolve his father.

An 18th-Century Madrid Crowd

As interesting as the miracle that forms the fresco's centrepiece, a typical Madrid crowd swarms around the saint. It was customary in such works that angels and cherubs appear in the cupola, above all the terrestrial activity, but Goya, never one to let himself be confined within the mores of the day, places the human above the divine.

Goya's Tomb

The painter is buried in front of the altar. His remains were transferred in 1919 from Bordeaux (France), where he had died in self-imposed exile in 1828. Oddly, the skeleton that was exhumed in Bordeaux was missing one important item – the head.

Nearby: Templo de Debod

Up the hill from the Ermita, this Egyptian **temple** (Paseo del Pintor Rosales; admission free; ⊙10am-8pm Tue-Sun; Ⓜ Ventura Rodríguez) was saved from the rising waters of Lake Nasser (Egypt) during the building of the Aswan Dam. After 1968 it was sent block by block to Spain as a gesture of thanks to Spanish archaeologists in the Unesco team that worked to save the monuments.

★ Top Tips

○ Check the opening hours as they vary from the official hours, particularly in July and August.

○ Take with you Robert Hughes' masterful biography, *Goya* (2003), for fascinating background information on this period of the painter's life.

○ The best time to visit is soon after opening time in the morning – the Ermita gets busier as the day wears on.

✕ Take a Break

Casa Mingo (☎ 91 547 79 18; www.casa mingo.es; Paseo de la Florida 34; raciones €2.70-11, pollo asado €11; ⊙11am-midnight; Ⓜ Príncipe Pío), next to the Ermita, is a well-known Asturian cider house. It focuses primarily on its signature dish of *pollo asado* (roast chicken) accompanied by a bottle of cider.

Worth a Trip 🔭
San Lorenzo de El Escorial

Home to the majestic (and Unesco World Heritage–listed) monastery and palace complex of San Lorenzo de El Escorial, this one-time royal getaway is one of Madrid's most worthwhile excursions. First built on the orders of King Felipe II in the 16th century as both a royal palace and as a mausoleum for Felipe's parents, Carlos I and Isabel, it's an extraordinary place filled with art and surrounded by glorious gardens.

📞 91 890 78 18

www.patrimonio
nacional.es

adult/concession €10/5,
guide/audioguide €4/3,
EU citizens free last 3
hours Wed & Thu

🕐 10am-8pm Apr-Sep, to
6pm Oct-Mar, closed Mon

Historical Background

As was the royal prerogative in those days, several villages were razed to make way for the massive project, which included a decadent royal palace and a mausoleum for Felipe's parents, Carlos I and Isabel. Architect Juan de Herrera, a towering figure of the Spanish Renaissance, oversaw the project.

First Steps

Resist the rush to the heart of the complex and linger over the monastery's main entrance on the western side of the complex. Above the gateway a statue of St Lawrence stands watch, holding a symbolic gridiron, the instrument of his martyrdom (he was roasted alive on one).

Patio de los Reyes

After passing St Lawrence and grimacing at his fate, you'll first enter the Patio de los Reyes (Patio of the Kings), which houses the statues of the six kings of Judah. Admiring these statues, it's difficult not to marvel at the arrogance of the Spanish royals who saw nothing amiss in comparing themselves to the great kings of the past.

Basilica

Directly ahead of the Patio de los Reyes lies the sombre basilica. As you enter, look up at the unusual flat vaulting by the choir stalls. Once inside the church proper, turn left to view Benvenuto Cellini's white Carrara marble statue of Christ crucified (1576) – it's one of the most underrated masterpieces of the complex.

El Greco

The remainder of the ground floor contains various treasures, including some tapestries and an El Greco painting. Impressive as the painting is, it's a far cry from El Greco's dream of decorating the whole complex; he actually came to Spain from Greece in 1577 hoping to

★ Top Tips

o Try and avoid coming on weekends when half of Madrid seems to turn up.

o Consider staying overnight in the town to really enjoy the village.

o The local tourist office website (www.sanlorenzoturismo.org) is good for surrounding attractions if you plan to make a day of it.

o Take the audioguide to really get the depth of experiences on offer.

✗ Take a Break

La Cueva (☎ 91 890 15 16; www.mesonlacueva.com; Calle de San Antón 4; mains €19-33; ⊙1-4pm & 9-11pm), has been around since 1768 and remains a bastion of traditional Castilian cooking.

Restaurante Charolés (☎ 91 890 59 75; www.charolesrestaurante.com; Calle Floridablanca 24; mains €17-24, cocido per person €30; ⊙1-4pm & 9pm-midnight) does grilled or roasted meats to perfection.

get a job decorating El Escorial, although Felipe II rejected him as a court artist.

Two Museums

After wondering at what might have been had El Greco been given a free hand, head downstairs to the northeastern corner of the complex. You pass through the Museo de Arquitectura and the Museo de Pinturaf. The former tells (in Spanish) the story of how the complex was built, the latter contains 16th- and 17th-century Italian, Spanish and Flemish art.

Up & Down

The route through the monastery takes you upstairs into a gallery known as the Palacio de Felipe II or Palacio de los Austrias. You'll then descend to the 17th-century Panteón de los Reyes (Crypt of the Kings), where almost all Spain's monarchs since Carlos I are interred. It's a sober, domed and slightly claustrophobic structure with royal tombs piled four-high around the walls. Backtracking a little, you're in the Panteón de los Infantes (Crypt of the Princesses), with its white marble tombs.

San Lorenzo de El Escorial

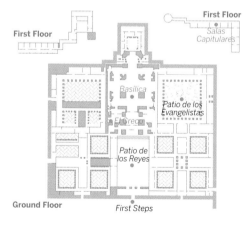

Developing a Royal Complex

This formidable palace-monastery complex was the brainchild of Spain's King Felipe II (r 1556–1598). Partly conceived as a decadent royal palace and as a mausoleum worthy of Felipe's parents, Carlos I and Isabel, El Escorial was also an announcement to increasingly Protestant Europe that Spain would always be Catholic.

As principal architect, Felipe II chose Juan Bautista de Toledo, who had worked on Rome's St Peter's Basilica. The architect's mission was, in the king's words, 'simplicity in the construction, severity in the whole, nobility without arrogance, majesty without ostentation.' In fulfilling these instructions, Juan Bautista de Toledo used locally quarried granite as the primary building material and followed a floor plan based on historical descriptions of Solomon's Temple in Jerusalem.

Several villages were razed to make way for the massive project and the first stone was laid in 1563 (two years after Madrid was chosen as Spain's capital). When Juan Bautista de Toledo died in 1567, architect Juan de Herrera, a towering figure of the Spanish Renaissance, took over the project and saw it through to completion in 1584.

Salas Capitilares

Stairs lead up from the cloistered Patio de los Evangelistas (Patio of the Gospels) to the Salas Capitulares (chapterhouses) in the southeastern corner of the monastery. These bright, airy rooms, whose ceilings are richly frescoed, contain a treasure chest of works by El Greco, Titian, Tintoretto, José de Ribera and Hieronymus Bosch (known as El Bosco to Spaniards).

Huerta de los Frailes

Just south of the monastery is the **Huerta de los Frailes** (Friars Garden; ☉10am-8pm Apr-Sep, to 6pm Oct-Mar, closed Mon), which merits a stroll. As royal gardens go, it's fairly modest, but can be a wonderfully tranquil spot when the rest of the complex is swarming with visitors.

Jardín del Príncipe

The **Prince's Garden** (admission free; ☉10am-8pm Apr-Sep, to 6pm Oct-Mar, closed Mon), which leads down to the town of El Escorial (and the train station), is a lovely monumental garden. It contains the **Casita del Príncipe** (www.patrimonionacional.es; €5; ☉10am-8pm Apr-Sep, to 6pm Oct-Mar, closed Mon), a little neo Classical gem built in 1772 by Juan de Villanueva under Carlos III for his heir, Carlos IV.

Survival Guide

Palacio de Cristal (p101), Parque del Buen Retiro
DAVID PEREIRAS/SHUTTERSTOCK ©

Before You Go

Book Your Stay

Madrid has high-quality accommodation at prices that haven't been seen in the centre of other European capitals in decades. Five-star temples to good taste and a handful of buzzing hostels bookend a fabulous collection of midrange hotels; most of the midrangers are creative originals, blending high levels of comfort with an often-quirky sense of style.

Useful Websites

EsMadrid.com (www.esmadrid.com) The tourist office website.

LeCool (http://madrid.lecool.com) Alternative, offbeat and avant-garde.

Lonely Planet (www.lonelyplanet.com/spain/madrid) An overview of Madrid with hundreds of useful links.

Turismo Madrid (www.turismomadrid.es) Regional Comunidad

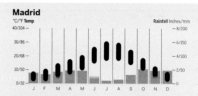

Madrid
°C/°F Temp   Rainfall Inches/mm

When to Go

Summer (Jun–Aug) Can be very hot; many locals leave the city; in August, many restaurants close and sights operate on reduced hours.

Autumn (Sep–Nov) Nice time to visit with mild temperatures; warmish in September, cool in November.

Winter (Dec–Feb) Can be bitterly cold; snow possible but often clear skies; Christmas is a festive time in the city; flamenco festival in February.

Spring (Mar–May) Mild temperatures; Semana Santa (Easter) and May festivals.

de Madrid tourist office site.

Madrid Diferente (www.madriddiferente.com) Offbeat guide to the city's attractions.

Best Budget

Madrid City Rooms (☎ 91 360 44 44; www.madridcityrooms.com; 2nd fl, Calle de la Cruz 6; s/d from €40/55; ❄ ☎ ; Ⓜ Sol) Outstanding service and excellent rooms in the centre.

Lapepa Chic B&B (☎ 648 474742; www.lapepa-bnb.com; 7th fl,

Plaza de las Cortes 4; s/d from €58/64; ❄ ☎ ; Ⓜ Banco de España) Fabulous budget B&B with attention to detail.

Hostal Main Street Madrid (☎ 91 548 18 78; www.mainstreetmadrid.com; 5th fl, Gran Vía 50; r from €55; ❄ ☎ ; Ⓜ Callao, Santo Domingo) Central and very cool *hostal*.

Flat 5 Madrid (☎ 91 127 24 00; www.flat5madrid.com; 5th fl, Calle de San Bernardo 55; s/d with private bathroom €55/70, r with shared bathroom from €48; ❄ 🛜; Ⓜ Noviciado) One of Madrid's best deals away from the tourist hordes.

Hostal Madrid (☎ 91 522 00 60; www.hostal-madrid.info; Calle de Esparteros 6; s €35-75, d €45-115, d apt €45-150; ❄ 🛜; Ⓜ Sol) Renovated rooms and friendly service downtown.

Best Midrange

Central Palace Madrid (☎ 91 548 20 18; www.centralpalacemadrid.com; Plaza de Oriente 2; d without/with view €90/160; ❄ 🛜; Ⓜ Ópera) Some of the best views in Madrid, whatever the price.

Posada del León de Oro (☎ 91 119 14 94; www.posadadelleondeoro.com; Calle de la Cava Baja 12; d/ste from €102/155; ❄ 🛜; Ⓜ La Latina) La Latina at its most atmospheric.

Catalonia Las Cortes (☎ 91 389 60 51; www.hoteles-catalonia.es; Calle del Prado 6; s/d from €150/175; ❄ 🛜; Ⓜ Antón Martín) Great rooms, service and Huertas location.

NH Collection Palacio de Tepa (☎ 91 389 64 90; www.nh-collection.com; Calle de San Sebastián 2; d from €175; ❄ 🛜; Ⓜ Antón Martín) Palace on the outside, stylish rooms within.

Praktik Metropol (☎ 91 521 29 35; www.praktikmetropol.com; Calle de la Montera 47; s/d from €90/100; ❄ 🛜; Ⓜ Gran Vía) Great views, cool rooms and fun atmosphere.

60 Balcones Recoletos (☎ 91 755 39 26; www.60balconies.com; Calle del Almirante 17; apt €132-212; ❄ 🛜; Ⓜ Chueca) Stylish apartments at the cool end of Chueca.

Best Top End

Hotel Orfila (☎ 91 702 77 70; www.hotelorfila.com; Calle de Orfila 6; r from €225; Ⓟ ❄ 🛜; Ⓜ Alonso Martínez) Unquestionable luxury with service to match.

Hotel Ritz (☎ 91 701 67 67; www.mandarinoriental.com; Plaza de la Lealtad 5; d/ste from €265/470; ❄ 🛜; Ⓜ Banco de España) Quite simply one of Europe's grandest hotels.

Villa Magna (☎ 91 587 12 34; www.villamagna.es; Paseo de la Castellana 22; d €335-420, ste from €450; Ⓟ ❄ 🛜; Ⓜ Rubén Darío) Refined Salamanca address for the well heeled.

Westin Palace (☎ 91 360 80 00; www.westinpalacemadrid.com; Plaza de las Cortes 7; d/ste from €200/470; ❄ 🛜; Ⓜ Banco de España, Antón Martín) Near faultless five-star address close to Paseo del Prado.

Hotel Urban (☎ 91 787 77 70; www.derbyhotels.com; Carrera de San Jerónimo 34; r from €230; ❄ 🛜 ♿; Ⓜ Sevilla) Swish downtown temple to modern luxury.

Arriving in Madrid

Adolfo Suárez Madrid-Barajas Airport

Metro (one way €4.50; 6.05am to 1.30am; 15 to 25 minutes; line 8) Runs to the Nuevos Ministerios transport interchange, which connects with lines 10 and 6. Buy tickets at the airport station.

Bus The Exprés Aeropuerto (Airport Express; www.emtmadrid.es; €5, 40 minutes; 24 hour) runs between Puerta de Atocha train station and the airport. From 11.30pm until 6am, departures are from the Plaza de Cibeles, not the train station.

Taxi A taxi to the centre (around 30 minutes, depending on traffic) costs a fixed €30.

Minibus AeroCITY (www.aerocity.com; 24 hour) is a private minibus service that takes you door-to-door between central Madrid and the airport. Prices vary according to the number of people but are generally cheaper than taxis.

Estación de Atocha

Metro (one-way/10-trip ticket €1.50/12.20; 6am to 1.30am; line 1) From Atocha Renfe station to Sol (10 to 15 minutes) with connections elsewhere via lines 2 and 3. Buy tickets from machines at the station.

Taxi A taxi to the centre (around 10 minutes, depending on traffic) costs €5 to €8, plus a €3 train-station supplement.

Estación de Chamartín

Metro (one-way/10-trip ticket €1.50/12.20; 6am-1am; lines 1 and 10) From Chamartín station to Sol station (15 to 20 minutes) with connections elsewhere via lines

Tickets & Passes

Tarjeta Multi

As of 1 January 2018, nonresidents travelling on the city's public transport system require a Tarjeta Multi, a rechargeable card that, unlike the resident's version, is not tied to your identity (ie neither your name nor your photo appears on the card). They can be purchased at machines in all metro stations, *estancos* (tobacconists) and other authorised sales points.

Like London's Oyster Card, you top up your account at machines in all metro stations and *estancos*, and touch-on and touch-off every time you travel. Options include 10 rides (bus and metro) for €12.20 or a single-journey option for €1.50.

Tarjeta Turística

The handy Tarjeta Turística (Tourist Pass) allows for unlimited travel on public transport across the Comunidad de Madrid (Community of Madrid) for tourists. You'll need to present your passport or national identity card and tickets can be purchased at all metro stations. Passes are available for 1/2/3/5/7 days for €8.40/14.20/18.40/26.80/35.40.

Emergency Numbers

To report thefts or other crime-related matters, your best bet is the **Servicio de Atención al Turista Extranjero** (Foreign Tourist Assistance Service; 📞91 548 85 37, 91 548 80 08; www.esmadrid.com/informacion-turistica/sate; Calle de Leganitos 19; 🕐9am-midnight; Ⓜ Plaza de España, Santo Domingo), which is housed in the central *comisaría* (police station) of the National Police. Here you'll find specially trained officers working alongside representatives from the Tourism Ministry. They can also assist in cancelling credit cards, as well as contacting your embassy or your family.

There's also a general number (📞902 102112; 24-hour English and Spanish, 8am to midnight other languages) for reporting crimes.

There's a **comisaría** (📞913 22 10 21; Calle de las Huertas 76; Ⓜ Antón Martín) down the bottom end of Huertas, near the Paseo del Prado.

2 and 3. Buy tickets from machines at the station.

Taxi A taxi to the centre (around 15 minutes, depending on traffic) costs around €10, plus a €3 train station surcharge.

Getting Around

Metro

○ Metro de Madrid (www.metromadrid.es) Runs a metro system with 11 colour-coded lines in central Madrid.

○ To travel on the metro you'll need to buy and charge up your Tarjeta Multi, or purchase a Tarjeta Turística.

○ Single journeys cost €1.50, while 10-trip tickets cost €12.20.

○ The metro operates from 6.05am to 1.30am.

Bus

○ Empresa Municipal de Transportes de Madrid (EMT) buses (www.emtmadrid.es) travel along most city routes regularly between about 6.30am and 11.30pm.

○ Twenty-six night-bus *búhos* (owls) routes operate from 11.45pm to 5.30am, with all routes originating in Plaza de la Cibeles.

Cercanías

○ The short-range *cercanías* trains operated by Renfe (www.renfe.es/cercanias/madrid) go places that the metro doesn't.

○ Tickets range between €1.70 and €8.70 depending on how far you're travelling.

Taxi

○ Taxis are reasonably priced and charges are posted on the inside of passenger-side windows. The trip from Sol to the Museo del Prado costs about €5.

○ You can call a taxi at Tele-Taxi (www.tele-taxi.es) and Radio-Teléfono Taxi (radiotelefono-taxi.com) or flag one down in the street.

Essential Information

Business Hours

Banks 8.30am–2pm Monday–Friday; some also open 4–7pm Thursday and 9am–1pm Saturday

Central Post Offices 8.30am–9.30pm Monday–Friday, 8.30am–2pm Saturday (most other branches 8.30am–2.30pm Monday–Friday, 9.30am–1pm Saturday)

Nightclubs midnight or 1am–5am or 6am

Restaurants Lunch 1–4pm, dinner 8.30–11pm or midnight

Shops 10am–2pm and 4.30–7.30pm or 5–8pm Monday–Saturday; some bigger shops don't close for lunch and many shops open on some Sundays, usually from 10am or 11am–7pm or 8pm

Supermarkets Big supermarkets and department stores generally open 10am–10pm Monday–Saturday

Dos & Don'ts

Greetings Greetings should precede even the most casual encounter – *hola, buenos días* is the perfect way to start.

Bars Don't be surprised to see people throwing their serviettes and olive stones on the floor – don't be the first to do it, but you might as well join in because a waiter will come around from time to time to sweep them all up.

Metro Stand on the right on escalators in metro stations.

Churches Unless you're there for religious reasons, avoid visiting churches (or taking photos) during Mass.

Bargaining Haggling is OK at El Rastro, but not the done thing elsewhere.

Money-Saving Tips

◦ Look out for free entry at sights.

◦ Order the *menú del día* (daily set menu) for lunch in restaurants.

Discount Cards

◦ The International Student Identity Card (ISIC; www.isic.org), the Euro<26 card (www.euro26.org) and (sometimes) university student cards entitle students to discounts of up to 50% at many sights.

◦ If you're over 65, you may be eligible for an admission discount to some attractions. Some attractions limit discounts to those with a Seniors Card issued by an EU country or other country with which Spanish citizens enjoy reciprocal rights.

◦ If you plan to visit the Museo del Prado, Museo Thyssen-Bornemisza and Centro de Arte Reina Sofía, the Paseo del Arte ticket covers them all in a combined ticket (€29.60) and is valid for one visit to each gallery during a 12-month period.

Electricity

Type C
220V/230V/50Hz

Money

o **Currency** Euro (€)

o **ATMs** Widely available; usually a charge on ATM cash withdrawals abroad.

o **Cash** Banks and building societies offer the best rates; take your passport. Credit cards Accepted in most hotels, restaurants and shops; may need to show passport or other photo ID.

o **Tipping** Small change in restaurants, round up to the nearest euro in taxis.

Public Holidays

Madrid's 14 public holidays are as follows:

Año Nuevo (New Year's Day) 1 January

Reyes (Epiphany or Three Kings' Day) 6 January

Jueves Santo (Holy Thursday) March/April

Viernes Santo (Good Friday) March/April

Labour Day (Fiesta del Trabajo) 1 May

Fiesta de la Comunidad de Madrid 2 May

Fiestas de San Isidro Labrador 15 May

La Asunción (Feast of the Assumption) 15 August

Día de la Hispanidad (Spanish National Day) 12 October

Todos los Santos (All Saints' Day) 1 November

Día de la Virgen de la Almudena 9 November

Día de la Constitución (Constitution Day) 6 December

La Inmaculada Concepción (Feast of the Immaculate Conception) 8 December

Navidad (Christmas) 25 December

Safe Travel

Madrid is generally safe, but as in any large European city, keep an eye on your belongings and exercise common sense.

o El Rastro, around the Museo del Prado and the metro are favourite pickpocketing haunts, as are any areas where tourists congregate in large numbers.

o Avoid park areas (such as the Parque del Buen Retiro) after dark.

o Keep a close eye on your taxi's meter and try to keep track of the route to make sure you're not being taken for a ride.

Toilets

Public toilets are almost nonexistent in Madrid and it's not really the done thing to go into a bar or cafe solely to use the toilet; ordering a quick coffee is a small price to pay for relieving the problem. Otherwise you can usually get away with it in a larger, crowded place where they can't really keep track of who's coming and going.

Another option is the department stores of El Corte Inglés that are dotted around the city.

Tourist Information

Centro de Turismo de Madrid (☎ 010, 91 578 78 10; www.esmadrid. com; Plaza Mayor 27; ⏰ 9.30am-8.30pm; **M** Sol) The Madrid government's Centro de Turismo is terrific.

Centro de Turismo Colón (www.esmadrid. com; Plaza de Colón 1; ⏰ 9.30am-8.30pm; **M** Colón) A smaller tourist office accessible via the underground stairs on the corner of Calle de Goya and Paseo de la Castellana.

Punto de Información Turística CentroCentro (☎ 91 578 78 10; www.esmadrid.com; Plaza de la Cibeles 1; ⏰ 10am-8pm Tue-Sun; **M** Banco de España)

Punto de Información Turística Plaza de Callao (www.esmadrid. com; Plaza de Callao; ⏰ 9.30am-8.30pm; **M** Callao)

Punto de Información Turística Paseo del Prado (☎ 91 578 78 10; www.esmadrid.com; Plaza de Neptuno; ⏰ 9.30am-8.30pm; **M** Atocha)

Punto de Información Turística Adolfo Suárez Madrid-Barajas T2 (www.es madrid.com; between Salas 5 & 6; ⏰ 9am-8pm)

Punto de Información Turística Adolfo Suárez Madrid-Barajas T4 (www. esmadrid.com; Salas 10 & 11; ⏰ 9am-8pm)

Travellers with Disabilities

○ Go to the section of the Madrid tourist office website known as Accessible Madrid (www. esmadrid.com/ en/madridaccesible), where you can download a pdf of their excellent, 421-page *Guia* *de Turismo Accesible in English or Spanish*. It has an exhaustive list of the city's attractions and transport and a detailed assessment of their accessibility, as well as a list of accessible restaurants.

○ For hotels and *hostales*, go to 'Alojamientos Accesibles' to download the website's similarly excellent *Guia de Alojamiento Accesible*.

○ Download Lonely Planet's free Accessible Travel guide from http://lptravel.to/ AccessibleTravel.

Visas

○ Citizens or residents of EU and Schengen countries: no visa required.

○ Citizens or residents of Australia, Canada, Israel, Japan, NZ and the USA: no visa required for tourist visits of up to 90 days every six months.

○ Other countries: check with a Spanish embassy or consulate.

Language

Spanish (*español*) – often referred to as *castellano* (Castilian) to distinguish it from other languages spoken in Spain – is the language of Madrid. While you'll find an increasing number of *madrileños* (people from Madrid) who speak some English, especially younger people and hotel and restaurant employees, don't count on it. Travellers who learn a little Spanish will be amply rewarded as Spaniards appreciate the effort, no matter how basic your understanding of the language.

Most Spanish sounds are pronounced the same as their English counterparts. Just read our pronunciation guides as if they were English and you'll be understood. Note that 'm/f' indicates masculine and feminine forms.

To enhance your trip with a phrasebook, visit **lonelyplanet. com**. Lonely Planet iPhone phrasebooks are available through the Apple App store.

Basics

Hello.
Hola. · o·la

Goodbye.
Adiós. · a·dyos

How are you?
¿Qué tal? · ke tal

Fine, thanks.
Bien, gracias. · byen gra·thyas

Please.
Por favor. · por fa·vor

Thank you.
Gracias. · gra·thyas

Excuse me.
Perdón. · per·don

Sorry.
Lo siento. · lo syen·to

Yes./No.
Sí./No. · see/no

Do you speak (English)?
¿Habla (inglés)? · a·bla (een·gles)

I (don't) understand.
Yo (no) entiendo. · yo (no) en·tyen·do

What's your name?
¿Cómo se · ko·mo se
llama? · lya·ma

My name is ...
Me llamo ... · me lya·mo ...

Eating & Drinking

Can I see the menu, please?
¿Puedo ver el · pwe·do ver el
menu, por favor? · me·noo por fa·vor

I'm a vegetarian. (m/f)
Soy · soy
vegetariano/a. · ve·khe·ta·rya·no/a

Cheers!
¡Salud! · sa·loo

That was delicious!
¡Estaba · es·ta·ba
buenísimo! · bwe·nee·see·mo

The bill, please.
La cuenta, · la kwen·ta
por favor. · por fa·vor

I'd like ...
Quisiera ... · kee·sye·ra ...

a coffee · *un café* · oon ka·fe

a table · *una mesa* · oo·na me·sa
for two · *para dos* · pa·ra dos

a wine · *un vino* · oon vee·no

two beers · *dos* · dos
· *cervezas* · ther·ve·thas

Shopping

I'd like to buy ...
Quisiera   kee·sye·ra
comprar ...   kom·prar ...

Can I look at it?
¿Puedo verlo?   pwe·do ver·lo

How much is it?
¿Cuánto cuesta?   kwan·to kwes·ta

That's very expensive.
Es muy caro.   es mooy ka·ro

Can you lower the price?
¿Podría bajar   po·dree·a
ba·khar
un poco   oon po·ko
el precio?   el pre·thyo

Emergencies

Help!
¡Socorro!   so·ko·ro

Call a doctor!
¡Llame a   lya·me a oon
un médico!   me·dee·ko

Call the police!
¡Llame a   lya·me a
la policía!   la po·lee·thee·a

I'm lost. (m/f)
Estoy perdido/a.   es·toy
per·dee·do/a

I'm ill. (m/f)
Estoy enfermo/a.   es·toy en·fer·mo/a

Where are the toilets?
¿Dónde están   don·de es·tan
los baños?   los ba·nyos

Time & Numbers

What time is it?
¿Qué hora es?   ke o·ra es

It's (10) o'clock.
Son (las diez).   son (las dyeth)

morning	*mañana*	ma·nya·na
afternoon	*tarde*	tar·de
evening	*noche*	no·che

yesterday	*ayer*	a·yer
today	*hoy*	oy
tomorrow	*mañana*	ma·nya·na

1	*uno*	oo·no
2	*dos*	dos
3	*tres*	tres
4	*cuatro*	kwa·tro
5	*cinco*	theen·ko
6	*seis*	seys
7	*siete*	sye·te
8	*ocho*	o·cho
9	*nueve*	nwe·ve
10	*diez*	dyeth

Transport & Directions

Where's ...?
¿Dónde está ...?   don·de es·ta ...

Where's the station?
¿Dónde está   don·de es·ta
la estación?   la es·ta·thyon

What's the address?
¿Cuál es la   kwal es la
dirección?   dee·rek·thyon

Can you show me (on the map)?
¿Me lo puede   me lo pwe·de
indicar   een·dee·kar
(en el mapa)?   (en el ma·pa)

I want to go to ...
Quisiera ir a ...   kee·sye·ra eer a ...

What time does it arrive/leave?
¿A qué hora   a ke o·ra
llega/sale?   lye·ga/sa·le

Please tell me when we get to ...
¿Puede avisarme   pwe·de a·vee·sar·me
cuando lleguemos   kwan·do lye·ge·mos
a ...?   a ...

I want to get off here.
Quiero bajarme   kye·ro ba·khar·me
aquí.   a·kee

Index

See also separate subindexes for:
Eating p157
Drinking p158
Entertainment p158
Shopping p158

Sights 000
Map Pages **000**

Behind the Scenes

Send Us Your Feedback

We love to hear from travellers – your comments help make our books better. We read every word, and we guarantee that your feedback goes straight to the authors. Visit **lonelyplanet.com/contact** to submit your updates and suggestions.

Note: We may edit, reproduce and incorporate your comments in Lonely Planet products such as guidebooks, websites and digital products, so let us know if you don't want your comments reproduced or your name acknowledged. For a copy of our privacy policy visit lonelyplanet.com/privacy.

Anthony's Thanks

A life built in Spain encompasses so many relationships that extend far beyond one trip. Heartfelt thanks to Sandra, Javi, Dani, Lucia, Marina, Alberto, Jose, Bea and so many others. *Gracias* also to Eli Morales. At Lonely Planet, I am grateful to my destination editor Tom Stainer and numerous editors who brought focus and much wisdom to the book. To my family – Marina, Carlota and Valentina – who have always made Madrid a true place of the heart: *con todo mi amor*. And to Jan, we hope to see you in Madrid again soon.

Acknowledgements

Cover photograph: Palacio de Cristal, Parque del Buen Retiro, Stefano Politi Markovina/AWL ©

Photographs pp30-1 (from left): emperorcosar/Shutterstock; Alex Segre/Alamy Stock Photo; Brian Kinney/Shutterstock; LucVi/Shutterstock

This Book

This 5th edition of Lonely Planet's *Pocket Madrid* guidebook was curated, researched and written by Anthony Ham, who also wrote the previous edition. This guidebook was produced by the following:

Destination Editor Tom Stainer

Senior Product Editor Genna Patterson

Product Editor Jenna Myers

Senior Cartographer Anthony Phelan

Book Designer Mazzy Prinsep

Assisting Editors Bruce Evans, Gabby Innes

Assisting Cartographer Valentina Kremenchutskaya

Assisting Book Designer Meri Blazevski

Cover Researcher Naomi Parker

Thanks to Hans Peter Graf, Anne Mason, Kate Mathews, Paul McEvoy

Our Writer

Anthony Ham

Anthony is a freelance writer and photographer who specialises in Spain, East and Southern Africa, the Arctic and the Middle East. When he's not writing for Lonely Planet, Anthony writes about and photographs Spain, Africa and the Middle East for newspapers and magazines in Australia, the UK and US. In 2001, after years of wandering the world, Anthony finally found his spiritual home when he fell irretrievably in love with Madrid on his first visit to the city. Less than a year later, he arrived there on a one-way ticket, with not a word of Spanish and not knowing a single person in the city. When he finally left Madrid ten years later, Anthony spoke Spanish with a Madrid accent, was married to a local and Madrid had become his second home. Now back in Australia, Anthony continues to travel the world in search of stories.

Published by Lonely Planet Global Limited
CRN 554153
5th edition – Dec 2018
ISBN 978 1 78657 278 3
© Lonely Planet 2018   Photographs © as indicated 2018
10 9 8 7 6 5 4 3 2 1
Printed in Malaysia